W9-CXO-558

𝔚𝔈 are beings from another dimension

everything you always wanted

(and how to get it)

Michael B. Malvin

Illustrations by Leslie Tryon-Tatoian
Photography by Buddy Rosenberg/Bob Levy

A **DREAMWORLD**™ Publication   **Los Angeles, California**

© 1977 Michael B. Malvin

All rights reserved. No part of this publication may be reproduced or transmitted in any form or by any means, electronic or mechanical, including without limitation, photocopy, recording, or any information storage and retrieval system, without permission in writing from the publisher.

ISBN 0-89624-873-9

Library of Congress Catalog Card Number: 77-23660

Printed in the United States of America

WEBSTER PERSONALITY GRADIENT™

SECTION I—STATISTICAL DATA

LAST NAME   FIRST NAME   MIDDLE INITIAL

STREET ADDRESS   APT. NO.

CITY   STATE   ZIP

Age ☐☐

Sex
☐ Female
☐ Male

Education
☐ High school or less
☐ Some college
☐ Bachelor's Degree
☐ Graduate School

Annual Income
☐ Less than $10,000
☐ $10,000–$15,000
☐ $15,000–$25,000
☐ more than $25,000

Marital Status
☐ Married
☐ Single
☐ Divorced
☐ Living with someone

Date ☐☐ ☐☐ ☐☐
Month Day Year

Do not write below this line

$\lambda_1 = $ ☐☐ $\lambda_4 = $ ☐☐ $\varrho = $ ☐☐
$\lambda_2 = $ ☐☐ $\varrho_\alpha = $ ☐☐ $\Sigma_x = $ ☐☐
$\lambda_3 = $ ☐☐ $\varrho_\beta = $ ☐☐ $\Sigma_\gamma = $ ☐☐

SECTION II—RESPONSES

1. A☐ B☐ C☐
2. A☐ B☐ C☐ D☐ E☐
3. A☐ B☐ C☐ D☐ E☐
4. A☐ B☐ C☐
5. A☐ B☐ C☐ D☐
6. A☐ B☐ C☐
7. A☐ B☐ C☐
8. A☐ B☐ C☐
9. A☐ B☐ C☐ D☐ E☐
10. A☐ B☐ C☐ D☐ E☐
11. A☐ B☐
12. A☐ B☐
13. A☐ B☐
14. A☐ B☐
15. A☐ B☐ C☐
16. A☐ B☐
17. A☐ B☐ C☐ D☐
18. A☐ B☐
19. A☐ B☐ C☐
20. A☐ B☐
21. A☐ B☐ C☐
22. A☐ B☐
23. A☐ B☐
24. A☐ B☐ C☐ D☐
25. A☐ B☐

26. A☐ B☐
27. A☐ B☐ C☐
28. A☐ B☐ C☐
29. A☐ B☐
30. A☐ B☐
31. A☐ B☐ C☐ D☐
32. A☐ B☐
33. A☐ B☐
34. A☐ B☐ C☐ D☐
35. A☐ B☐ C☐
36. A☐ B☐ C☐ D☐ E☐
37. A☐ B☐
38. A☐ B☐ C☐ D☐ E☐
39. A☐ B☐
40. A☐ B☐ C☐ D☐
41. A☐ B☐ C☐
42. A☐ B☐ C☐ D☐ E☐
43. A☐ B☐ C☐ D☐
44. A☐ B☐ C☐ D☐
45. A☐ B☐
46. A☐ B☐ C☐ D☐ E☐
47. A☐ B☐ C☐
48. A☐ B☐ C☐
49. A☐ B☐ C☐
50. A☐ B☐

turn page ➡

	A	B				A	B	C	
51.	☐	☐			76.	☐	☐	☐	

	A	B	C			A	B	C	
52.	☐	☐	☐		77.	☐	☐	☐	
53.	☐	☐	☐		78.	☐	☐	☐	

	A	B				A	B	C	
54.	☐	☐			79.	☐	☐	☐	
55	☐	☐			80.	☐	☐	☐	

	A	B	C			A	B	C	
56.	☐	☐	☐		81.	☐	☐	☐	
57.	☐	☐	☐		82.	☐	☐	☐	
58.	☐	☐	☐		83.	☐	☐	☐	

	A	B	C			A	B		
59.	☐	☐	☐		84.	☐	☐		

	A	B	C			A	B	C	
60.	☐	☐	☐		85.	☐	☐	☐	

	A	B	C				A	B	C	D
61.	☐	☐	☐			86.	☐	☐	☐	☐

	A	B	C			A	B	C	
62.	☐	☐	☐		87.	☐	☐	☐	

	A	B	C				A	B	C	D
63.	☐	☐	☐			88.	☐	☐	☐	☐

	A	B					A	B	C	D
64.	☐	☐				89.	☐	☐	☐	☐

	A	B	C			A	B	C	
65.	☐	☐	☐		90.	☐	☐	☐	

	A	B				A	B		
66.	☐	☐			91.	☐	☐		

	A	B	C	D			A	B	C	
67.	☐	☐	☐	☐		92.	☐	☐	☐	

	A	B	C	D			A	B		
68.	☐	☐	☐	☐		93.	☐	☐		

	A	B				A	B		
69.	☐	☐			94.	☐	☐		

	A	B					A	B	C	D
70.	☐	☐				95.	☐	☐	☐	☐

	A	B	C	D			A	B	C	D
71.	☐	☐	☐	☐		96.	☐	☐	☐	☐

	A	B					A	B	C	D
72.	☐	☐				97.	☐	☐	☐	☐

	A	B				A	B		
73.	☐	☐			98.	☐	☐		

	A	B					A	B	C	D
74.	☐	☐				99.	☐	☐	☐	☐

	A	B	C	D			A	B	
75.	☐	☐	☐	☐		100.	☐	☐	

this book is dedicated to you,
the most beautiful person
in the world

everything you always wanted™

TABLE OF CONTENTS

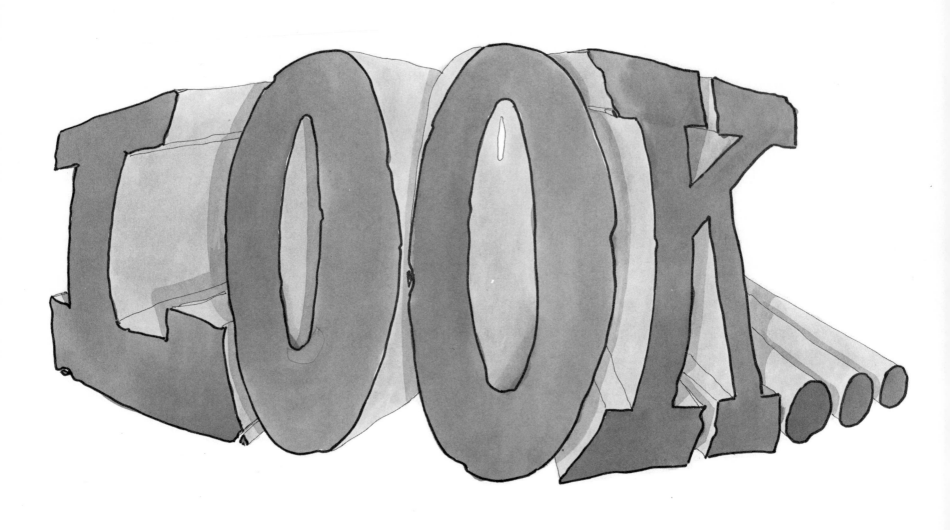

are ducked up

you believe
that the pale reflection
you saw in the mirror
is the real you.

THIS IS BULLSHIT!

You are more than you ever dreamed of.

You are the one
the only one
that exists.

YOU ARE THE MOST BEAUTIFUL PERSON IN THE WORLD

Remember it . . .

WEBSTER
PERSONALITY
GRADIENT™

WEBSTER PERSONALITY GRADIENT

What Is It? . . .

The Webster Personality Gradient is a psychometric association and preference index designed to help you better understand yourself.

What Does This Mean? . . .

The Webster Personality Gradient is designed to measure your own personal opinions, preferences and choices. Basically, there are no "right" or "wrong" answers, only your own opinion.

How Will It Help? . . .

Your answer sheet will be put through a computer which will produce a personalized analysis for you, based upon your own individual responses.

This personalized analysis will help you by suggesting possible areas for you to concentrate on to build yourself up.

INSTRUCTIONS FOR TAKING THE WEBSTER PERSONALITY GRADIENT

Materials Needed

A number 2 pencil with eraser

Time Limit

The Webster Personality Gradient has no time limit, but do complete the entire test at one sitting.

Response Sheet

Everything You Always Wanted contains a perforated, tear-out response sheet in the front of the book. Carefully remove it.

Statistical Data

Neatly print all the information called for in the statistical data section.

Sample Response

When you have chosen your response to a question, carefully and completely fill in the box corresponding to your choice.

	A	B	C	D	E
Sample	□	□	■	□	□

Do not put "x" or "✓". Respond only as shown above.

Where To Send the Test

Send the test and a stamped self-addressed envelope to:

EYAW
North American Test Center
Box 67608
Los Angeles, CA 90067

If you do not comply fully with the above instructions, your test cannot be processed.

1. **Which woman do you identify most with?**

   Ⓐ Barbra Streisand
   Ⓑ Joan of Arc
   Ⓒ Helen Gurley Brown

2. **Choose one of the following numbers:**

   Ⓐ 9
   Ⓑ 13
   Ⓒ 21
   Ⓓ 666
   Ⓔ 1,000

3. **Choose one:**

   Ⓐ R
   Ⓑ L
   Ⓒ W
   Ⓓ G
   Ⓔ K

4. **Everyone is equal.**

   Ⓐ True
   Ⓑ False
   Ⓒ No opinion

5. **Color in any triangle.**

   Ⓐ a
   Ⓑ b
   Ⓒ c
   Ⓓ d

6. **This is:**

   Ⓐ The figure "8"
   Ⓑ A mobius band
   Ⓒ The sign for infinity

7. **Pick one word that best describes the ideal man:**

   Ⓐ Sexy
   Ⓑ Understanding
   Ⓒ Rich

8. **Pick one word that best describes the ideal woman:**

   Ⓐ Sexy
   Ⓑ Rich
   Ⓒ Understanding

9. How often do you engage in sex?

    A Once a week
    B Twice a week
    C Three times a week
    D More frequently
    E Rarely or never

10. Choose one:

    A R . . . $19
    B L . . . $13
    C W . . . $21
    D G . . . $666
    E K . . . $1,000

11. If you saw an article in a store, mismarked for way less than its obvious value, would you try and get it for that price?

    A No
    B Yes

12. When you loan something to a friend, do you keep close track of it?

    A Yes
    B No

13. Do you bite your fingernails or chew on pencils?

    A No
    B Yes

14. Are you easy to please?

    A No
    B Yes

15. Do you feel that your opinions are correct, even though you may not be an expert in the field in question?

    A Sometimes
    B Usually
    C Infrequently

16. "Most people like me."

    A True
    B False

17. Circle as many colors as you can find.

```
B L A C K P O R O A
E O R N A N E O L Q
I Z I O E L M Y I U
G P A E M E I E V A
E E R P U A L L E M
L G L L O Y R L D A
R N E N A T G O L R
R A E R U S T W O I
U R G E T I H W G N
P O W D E R B L U E
```

    A 0   B 1 or 2   C 3 or 4   D 5 or more

18. Do you go to bed at a certain time, rather than when you feel sleepy?

    A No

    B Yes

19. Do you laugh?

    A Sometimes

    B Usually

    C Infrequently

20. Do you get upset if you cannot achieve what you set out to do?

    A No

    B Yes

21. Circle the figure most unlike the others.

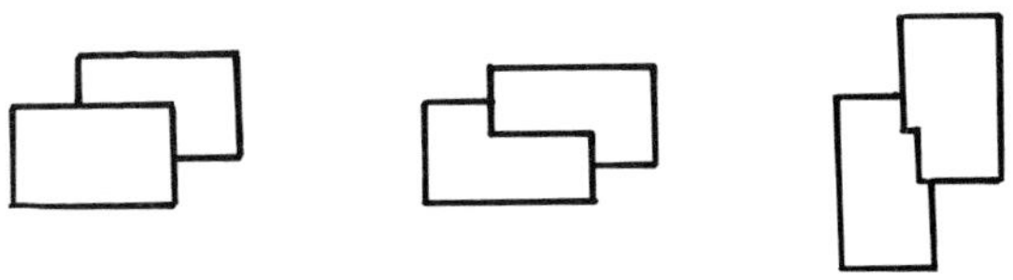

    A   B   C

22. Do you consider yourself generous?

    A Yes

    B No

23. Would your friends call you a leader?

    A No

    B Yes

24. How many foreign languages do you speak?

    A 0

    B 1

    C 2

    D 3 or more

25. Do you think about death or illness?

    A Yes

    B No

26. Do your muscles ever twitch without reason?

    A Yes

    B No

27. Which man do you identify most with?

    A Abraham Lincoln

    B J. Paul Getty

    C Elvis Presley

28. Choose one:

    Ⓐ The Beatles
    Ⓑ Doc Severinson
    Ⓒ Helen Reddy

29. Are you very fond of plants?

    Ⓐ Yes
    Ⓑ No

30. Do your neighbors like you?

    Ⓐ No
    Ⓑ Yes

31. Choose the two that are identical.

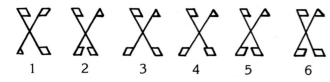

    Ⓐ 1 and 3
    Ⓑ 1 and 2
    Ⓒ 2 and 5
    Ⓓ none of the above

32. Do you like to drive fast?

    Ⓐ Yes
    Ⓑ No

33. Pick a pair of ducks.

Ⓐ

Ⓑ

34. Are you:

    Ⓐ Married
    Ⓑ Single
    Ⓒ Divorced
    Ⓓ None of the above

35. Would you rather be:

    Ⓐ Married
    Ⓑ Single
    Ⓒ Divorced

36. Put a check mark in one of the squares.

Ⓐ ☐ ☐ ☐
☐ Ⓑ ☐ Ⓒ
☐ ☐ ☐
☐ ☐ ☐
Ⓓ ☐ Ⓔ ☐

37. Do you enjoy wearing fashionable clothing?

A Yes
B No

38. Choose one.

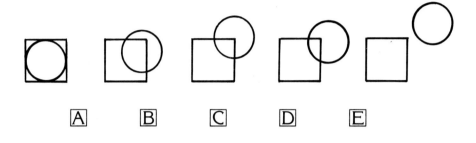

A   B   C   D   E

39. Do you consider yourself sexy?

A Yes
B No

40. Choose the two that are identical:

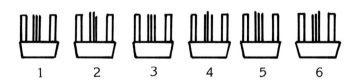

1   2   3   4   5   6

A 4 and 5
B 1 and 2
C 1 and 3
D 5 and 6

41. How often do you eat within two hours of going to sleep?

A Never
B Sometimes
C Usually

42. How many cubes are there in the figure.

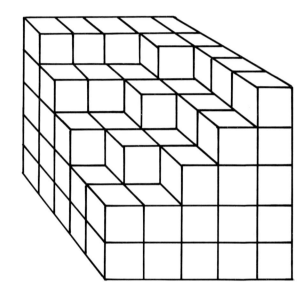

A 86
B 92
C 96
D 100
E none of the above

43. Choose your favorite color:

A Red
B Orange
C Yellow
D Blue

44. Choose a time of day.

    A 6 P.M.
    B 6 A.M.
    C noon
    D midnight

45. This is a floor plan of a spaceship. Would you rather live in:

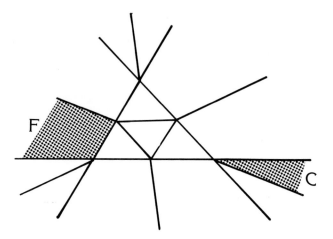

    A Room C
    B Room F

46. Which is the longest line?

    A 1
    B 2
    C 3
    D 4
    E 5

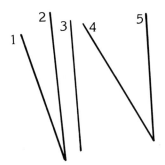

47. Do you worry about what people think of you?

    A Sometimes
    B Infrequently
    C Frequently

48. Do you wonder where your money has gone?

    A Infrequently
    B Sometimes
    C Often

49. Do you speak slowly and softly?

    A Often
    B Sometimes
    C Infrequently

50. Do you enjoy watching members of the opposite sex?

    A Yes
    B No

51. If you had to walk a distance because your friend didn't pick you up in a car, as promised, would you be angry?

    A Yes
    B No

52. Are you irritated by children?

    A Infrequently
    B Frequently
    C Sometimes

53. Do you think about your past failures?

    A Frequently
    B Sometimes
    C Infrequently

54. Choose one:

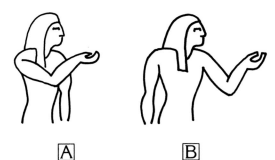

    A   B

55. Is your sex life satisfactory to you?

    A Yes
    B No

56. Which would you rather receive as a gift from a friend?

    A A book
    B An aquarium
    C A gift certificate

57. Choose one.

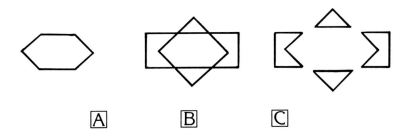

    A   B   C

58. In the above diagram, which shape most suggests value?

    A Figure A
    B Figure B
    C Figure C

59. Which attribute do you most associate with money?

    A Independence
    B Power
    C Fame

60. Which one of these forms most suggest autonomy to you?

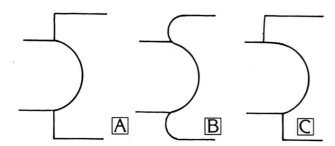

In the following two questions, choose the word pairs that are best related.

61. Space is to regal as platitude is to:

    Ⓐ epigram

    Ⓑ witicism

    Ⓒ hyperbole

62. Tropical is to forensic as jungle is to:

    Ⓐ monkey

    Ⓑ circumlocution

    Ⓒ judge

63. Choose the pair that are most related.

    Ⓐ a and b

    Ⓑ b and e

    Ⓒ d and e

64. Which do you value more?

    Ⓐ monetary possessions

    Ⓑ controlling your own thoughts.

65. Would you consider yourself spineless weakling if you permitted others to do your thinking for you?

    Ⓐ Yes

    Ⓑ Sometimes

    Ⓒ No

66. Choose one:

    Ⓐ   Ⓑ

67. Which dot would you choose?

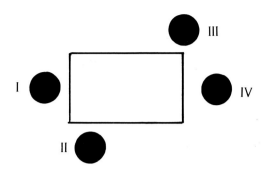

A I
B II
C III
D IV

68. Which of these illustrations is most sexually suggestive?

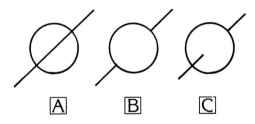

A   B   C

69. Are you really "close" with only a few people?

A No
B Yes

70. Can you "break the ice" at a party?

A Yes
B No

71. Pick the arrow that most appeals to you.

A
B
C
D

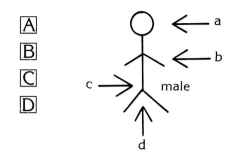

72. Do you often keep things because they may be useful at a later date.

A Yes
B No

73. Can you feel whatever emotion you desire?

A No
B Yes

74. Do people talk behind your back?

A Yes
B No

75. Pick the two that are the most dissimilar:

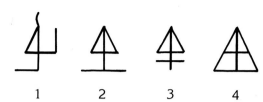

1   2   3   4

- [A] 1 and 3
- [B] 2 and 3
- [C] 1 and 4
- [D] None of the above

76. Which of these is most important to you?

- [A] A good income
- [B] A happy marriage
- [C] A large family

77. Which pair are most alike.

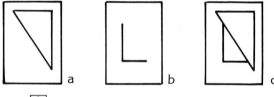

a   b   c

- [A] a and c
- [B] b and c
- [C] a and b

78. In the above illustration, which figure most suggests power?

- [A] a
- [B] b
- [C] c

79. Choose one:

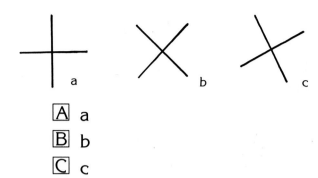

a   b   c

- [A] a
- [B] b
- [C] c

In the following series of numbers, choose the next number in each series:

80. 1, 2, 4 . . .

- [A] 8
- [B] 6
- [C] 16

81. 1, 2, 8 . . .

- [A] 18
- [B] 16
- [C] 14
- [D] none of the above

82. 27, 8, 1 . . .

- [A] −2
- [B] 0
- [C] none of the above

83. Are you the master of your own life?

  A Yes
  B Sometimes
  C No

84. Do you wish you had more money.

  A Yes
  B No

85. Do you ever boast or brag.

  A Yes
  B No
  C Sometimes

86. Choose the figure that best represents the word "future."

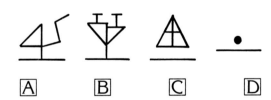

  A   B   C   D

87. Choose the figure that best represents the word "tolerance."

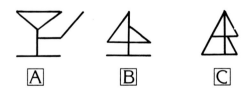

  A   B   C

88. Pick the arrow that most appeals to you.

  A
  B
  C
  D

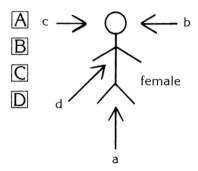

89. Which do you fear most?

  A Poverty
  B Ill health
  C Loneliness
  D Death

90. Which do you fear least?

  A Criticism
  B Poverty
  C Old age

91. Do you have trouble falling asleep?

  A Yes
  B No

92. Choose the figure that best represents the word "hostile."

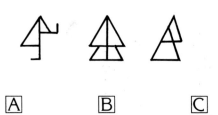

A B C

93. Pick the figure that looks happier.

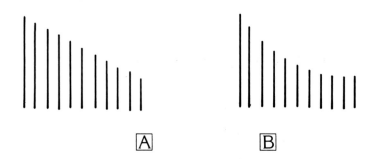

A B

94. Choose a set of squares.

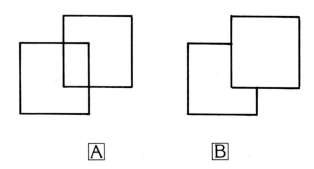

A B

The next three questions relate to the figures below:

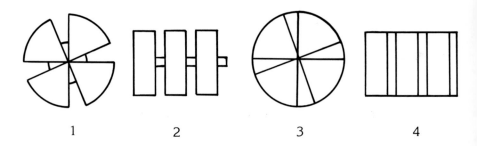

1 2 3 4

95. Choose the pair that are most alike.

A 1 and 3
B 2 and 4
C 3 and 4
D 2 and 3

96. Choose the pair that are most dissimilar.

A 1 and 3
B 2 and 4
C 3 and 4
D 2 and 3

97. Which of the figures most suggests communication?

A 1
B 2
C 3
D 4

98. Would you be concerned if you had to make a complete new start in your life.

    Ⓐ Yes

    Ⓑ No

99. Choose the figure that best represents "alienation."

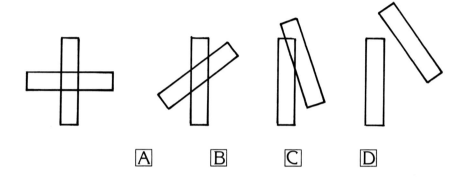

    Ⓐ   Ⓑ   Ⓒ   Ⓓ

100. Do you feel you are neat and organized?

    Ⓐ Yes

    Ⓑ No

Chapter 1

THE CHOICE OF LIFE

WHAT DOES THIS MEAN?

It means, no matter who we are in this entire universe, we all have exactly the same choice. We can choose to be happy or we can choose to be unhappy.

We alone make the choice. No one or nothing can keep us from being happy unless we allow it to.

It's so simple we lose sight of it.

INSTRUCTION No. 1

Make your choice . . .

Joe Yuga lives in the suburbs of Boston, Massachusetts with his wife and two kids. He makes a "nice living" working for a local aerospace company as an engineer. But like most of us, he's currently having trouble making ends meet. His company has just been taken over by a huge conglomerate and he's a bit concerned. Anything could happen. For example, this book could explode. He might be fired because of the takeover or perhaps promoted to a divisional manager; it's too early to tell. The last month has seen him become progressively uptight to the point where now he's nervous and irritable all the time. Joe is convinced that he has to please his boss. As a consequence, he sits at home and worries when he could be out enjoying a walk in the park with his children. Although it's obvious that worrying in no way affects the outcome of his dilemma and only wastes precious moments of existence, Joe can't seem to help himself. Although he has a station wagon, a cozy home in the suburbs, and most of the comforts of life, Joe never seems quite satisfied. He tends to feel that if he only had "a little more", things would be OK. This is a lie. Unless he becomes the master of his desires, Joe will be forever in need, walking a treadmill to oblivion.

The truth is, creation will endlessly serve up a new round of things to chase after, a new round of things to hunger for, and the relentless merry-go-round of insatiable desires will never stop—until we do.

Joe got fired.

Joe went home in a really lousey mood, argued with his wife, and spanked his five-year-old son needlessly with a toothpick. Walking down the street towards the local bar, he spots Richard Star driving a new $40,000 Rolls-Royce. Joe peers through the window to see a beautiful young "thing" throwing herself all over Richard. "Look at that rich, ego-tripping playboy", Joe says to himself, jealously. "Why does he deserve more than me; he's no better." Joe is really angry and confused. Richard Star is the High School janitor. Being alive is hell for Joe under these conditions. Just then a cement truck skids through a red light and smashes into the Rolls-Royce—two seconds later both the car and Richard Star are chicken soup.

Joe stands there and stares in disbelief. "I was so jealous of that guy two minutes ago and now he's dead. I sure wouldn't want to trade places with him now—stamps maybe, but not places." Joe is beginning to realize that his consciousness and existence are priceless. How could he have longed for something so temporary as Richard Star's wealth and power. How could he have so desperately desired something so easily destroyed. How could he be so caught up in chasing after the fleeting goals and cardboard images that our society is trying to pawn off on him. **How could he!** Read on and find out . . .

As Joe looks at Richard Star's dead body being hauled into the back of a waiting ambulance, there is one other thing he ponders. "Richard's body looks the same as it did when he was 'alive'. The body is the identical one that was driving the Rolls-Royce five minutes ago. Yet it definitely is not alive. What is missing that used to be there? Surely it's not part of his body because all the parts are still there." Except for his wallet, which mysteriously vanished along with the beautiful young "thing". Joe is beginning to understand that "death" simply means that the body no longer has awareness of its existence. The motivating force, the power that held it together as a thinking, conscious being, has simply gone elsewhere. "So", Joe says, "poor Star's dead, and I'm not. Boy, I can really use that drink now."

Joe is leaning over the bar, downing his second beer, when in comes a guy in a wheelchair being pushed by a nurse. Joe looks at the cripple, who spills his drink all over himself, and Joe feels genuinely sorry. "What a night," Joe says to himself. "I never stopped to think how lucky I am that my body works so well and that all the parts are there. Sure, I got laid off from my job, but look at Richard Star and now this guy. No, I wouldn't trade places with either of them—stamps maybe, but not places. I guess it was kind of silly to worry about getting laid off. All it did was cause me to be unhappy."

The guy in the wheelchair seems to have picked up on Joe's vibration. "Don't feel sorry for me, Buddy," the cripple says, "I used to be angry and resentful of all the things I didn't have, too, but now I count my blessings. There's guys down at the VA Hospital that don't have even arms or legs." Joe looks at the cripple, his clothes soaked with beer, and understands. With a tear in his eye, Joe pats the disabled man warmly on the shoulder and softly whispers in his ear . . . "Got any stamps?"

No matter who or where we are, there are always people "better off" and always people "worse off".

No matter who or where we are, there are always people "better off" and always people "worse off."

It is our choice to be happy or unhappy

with whatever creation gives us.

No one or nothing can "make us" unhappy except ourselves. It is our attitude that makes the difference. To be unhappy and say, "If only I had this or that, then I would be happy" is stupid. By desiring something that we think is missing from our lives, we are literally choosing to be unhappy and unfulfilled.

Although we all agree that choosing to be unhappy is totally stupid, we all do it in varying degrees. We dwell on the negative—what we don't have—instead of appreciating the positive which is all around us.

Is the Glass Half Empty or Half Full?

Chapter 2

TOWER OF POWER

There are forces in

the universe that cannot be

perceived by your five senses

A radio transmitter sends out electromagnetic signals that cannot be perceived by the human body

How many other such signals can you think of?

There are other finer forces, activities, processes, and functions in the universe that are beyond the power and ability of the physical body to contact or register. The microscope, telescope, and photographic lens are instruments demonstrating the existence of physical vibrations finer than the physical body is able to detect—vibrations literally beyond the limit of the five senses.

elec·tro·mag·net·ic body \i-lek-trō-ˈmag-net-ik ˈbäd-ē\ *n. pl* **bod·ies** [fr. Gk, *elektron;* ME, fr OE *bodig*]: the energy field centered in and radiating outward from the physical body.

Even now, it is a known fact that we have an Electromagnetic Body which emits detectable vibrations of energy. People instinctively reognize this. Consider expressions such as "she gives me good vibrations". With present-day instruments of "modern science", electromagnetic fields can be measured and defined beyond the limits of the physical body. We can even take pictures of them utilizing the techniques of Kirlian photography.[1]

---

[1] For those who are interested in this field, we suggest reading Pieirakos, J., "The Human Energy Field", **The Energies of Consciousness,** Krippner, S. (Ed.) and D. Rubin, Gorder and Breach, N.Y., pp. 157–167.

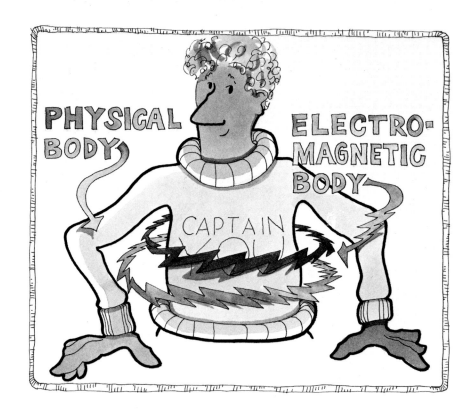

Here's you and the electromagnetic body.

Pictures of electromagnetic bodies using the technique of high voltage or Kirlian photography.

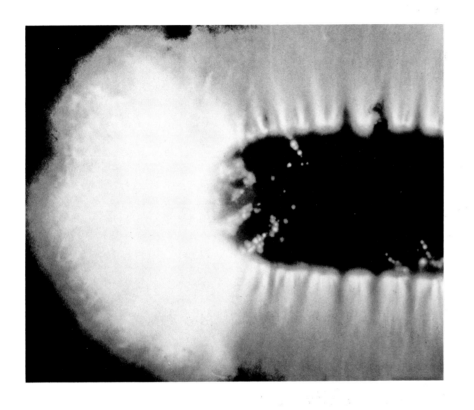

Electrophotograph, right index finger during state of rest.

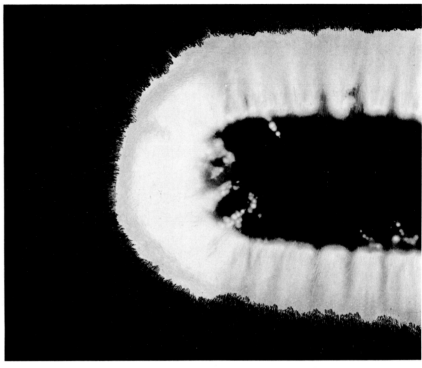

Electrophotograph, right index finger after sexual intercourse.

All living things possess an electromagnetic body.

**HERE ARE THE REASONS
WHY WE DON'T READILY
PERCEIVE THE
ELECTROMAGNETIC BODY:**

- **Emphasis on Material Consumption and Acquisition as Providing the Only Satisfactions in Life**

- **Vibrations of Increased Mechanization and Urbanization Drown Out the Finer Vibrations of the Electromagnetic Body**

- **Body Pollution, Chemicals, Junk Food Weaken Perception**

an electromagnetic pick-up . . .

Whether we realize it or not, each of us has encountered during our day-to-day living many examples of the perceptions of our own Electromagnetic Body.

For example, we've all experienced knowing what someone is thinking before they say it, or had premonitions of the future. ESP or psychic phenomena are nothing more than perception through the electromagnetic body. The physical body, by its very nature, cannot pick up vibrations beyond the limits of the five physical senses. The Electromagnetic Body, consisting of our electromagnetic force field which extends beyond the physical body, is capable of picking up perceptions generated beyond the range of the physical body.

If for example, our Electromagnetic Body extends five feet beyond the physical body and something happens three feet away, the electromagnetic body will pick up a sensation.

Here's the electromagnetic body picking up a sensation.

It is like a spider and his web. By means of his web (which we could consider a rough analogy to the "Electromagnetic Body in this case) the spider can pick up vibrations (perceptions) beyond his physical body.

When we learn how to perceive through our Electromagnetic Bodies we become aware of phenomena never before experienced through our physical bodies.

What is generally called intuition is electromagnetic perception, obtained through the electromagnetic body, just as physical sensation constitutes physical experience. As physically embodied human beings, we are not generally aware of the fact that we possess electromagnetic bodies although we function with and through them. Because we identify with the physical body and falsely believe it to be the sum total of our being, most of us have not yet learned how to identify and consciously experience the electromagnetic body with all the many wonders it holds for us.

Chapter 3

DEATH IS A FIVE LETTER WORD

the happy hunting grounds...

We as human beings fear death because we know that some day we must go to the happy hunting grounds. Unlike anything else (taxes included) of which there is always the possibility of avoiding, we know that all bodies wind up dead.

Our usual method of dealing with this "problem" is to either (a) not think about it because there is no sense in being "morbid", or (b) get lost in the empty performance of some set of rite and ritual which promises us a happier existence after we do die. Both of these approaches lead to continued anxiety, fear and frustration.

Although the dominant religions of the West preach the joys of the hereafter in such glorious terms that it would seem like every believer should welcome the transition; although it might well be supposed that relatives and friends would don gay robes and deck themselves with bright flowers to celebrate the passage of the loved one to a happier and brighter sphere of existence—we see just the opposite manifestation.

The average person, in spite of his faith and creed, seems to dread the approach of the "grim reaper"; his friends mourn and drape themselves in black giving every outward appearance of morbidity at having lost their loved one "forever", thereby being forcibly reminded of their own inevitable demise. In spite of their beliefs or expression of faith in eternal happiness with the coming of the hereafter, death has a terror they seemingly cannot overcome. Basically everyone is afraid to die. If anyone should boast otherwise, invite him for a quiet walk around the block after midnight.

When a child's mother dies, it stands before the mother's body crying because the mother is gone. But what is missing? The body is still there, but the spark of life, the intelligence that makes it "live" isn't there. This same intelligence, consciousness, call it what you like, is electromagnetic energy that during "life" is centered in the physical body. When death occurs, that electromagnetic energy is no longer centered in the physical body. "Death" means this and nothing more.

you are not your car . . .

The essence of achieving the power of life is understanding that although we are inextricably intertwined in the body while living on the material earth plane, we are more than just a bag of plasma and pus. . . . Our car is a useful vehicle, but we don't become so involved in driving it that we believe WE are the car. We understand that "we" are the intelligence behind the controls. Similarly, "Everything You Always Wanted" will reveal to you the real "you" —the Electromagnetic Body—the intelligence and consciousness that drives (the vehicle of) your body.

note:
in the interests of saving a few trees, we will sometimes write "Everything You Always Wanted as **"EYAW"**

The body is the car in which we ride down the highway of life.

life is constant change . . .

The nature of the universe is constant change and flux. The bodies we now inhabit and the electromagnetic energies associated with them are also constantly changing. Consider the relentless alteration (both physical and mental) that takes place while growing from an unborn fetus to a child, to a person of thirty, and finally to an elderly person of seventy-five. Because the body does not notice the transition day by day, it would like to think things aren't changing.

During life, our Electromagnetic Body undergoes continuous flux and permutation, just like the physical body. These changes are perceived by us as different states of mood and consciousness. These alterations are caused by the experience and actions of our lives in these bodies. For example, if our mood switches from happiness to anger, our electromagnetic energy field changes measurably even with today's crude instruments. After the event of death, the electromagnetic body is no longer centered in the physical body, but becomes part of the ambient universe. Just because the Electromagnetic Body is no longer centered in the physical body does not mean that it disappears or ceases to exist.

Life is constant change.

Since this electromagnetic energy continues to exist, although not centered in the body, it will continue by the very nature of its existence to have consciousness, even though this consciousness is not comprehended through the five physical senses of the body.

We fear because we mistakenly believe we are only the physical body. If we give up our habit of perceiving things only through the five senses of our present bodies and learn to identify ourselves with the electromagnetic body, we will become fearless; we will amass an expanded consciousness and perception, and perhaps a fortune.

$$E = MC^2$$

As Einstein proved, energy can neither be created nor destroyed, it can only change form.

Contrary to popular belief, giving up our attachment to the gratification of only the five senses and the idea that we are only the physical body does not mean we have "less." Quite the opposite, it means we can enjoy more levels of living in a physical body without having to hopelessly cling to a physical body that is inevitably going to grow old and crumble before our very eyes.

Isn't that something you always wanted?

Chapter 4

THE TELLTALE TONGUE

what you speak is what you get . . .

The words which emanate from the tongue are the measure of our true selves. If they're hateful, angry or judgmental, we cannot claim to be peaceful or happy.

If, on the other hand they are beautiful, calm and few, our words will be sought and respected.

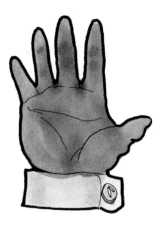

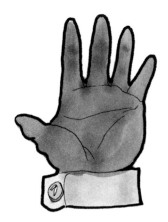

By exercising your power and control to change your speaking patterns, as we shall discuss below, you will feel immediate positive effects that will give you added self-confidence and personal power. Now,

Isn't that something you always wanted?

First Principle of Speaking:

speak less

Most people speak entirely too much. For whatever reason, whether it be because of nervousness, desire for attention, old habits, or lack of concentration, most of us are trying to talk too much. We would much rather talk than listen. Listening becomes a matter of sitting there "waiting" for our "turn" to speak.

The words we speak, the manner in which we project them, and the vibrations, auditory and otherwise, that we emit in conjunction with our speech are our "ambassadors", and should be chosen carefully.

avoid verbal inflation . . .

When the government prints up too much money, there are more pieces of paper around so each piece of paper is worth less—and eventually worthless. We all, of course, know this as "inflation".

Printing too much money causes it to be cheap (unless, of course, you're not the government).

Similarly, when our tongue "prints up" too many words, they become cheap. Words of people who talk too much are not valued. Words of those who speak infrequently **command instant attention** and are sought by others. If you value your words, so will others.

Make sense, not cents.

save energy . . .

Speaking requires a great deal of physical energy. While you can, of course, speak for hours if necessary, the long-term effect of needless speaking is a measurable decrease in physical energy. By speaking less you will, over a period of time, definitely add to your energy.

enjoy playing a game of power . . .

Try this strategy next time you are in a discussion with a group of people. Instead of inevitably preparing your next statement while others are speaking, say to yourself, "I'm going to have fun this time and not speak." Now, when others speak, don't be disinterested just because you aren't speaking. Look directly at each person as you listen and smile slightly, not necessarily a toothy grin, but utilize some sort of facial expression that conveys interest and caring. Engaging in eye contact will help you listen and relate in detail to the speaker with the added benefit of picking up many subtle undertones that your fellow listeners will miss. Since most of those around you will be on personal ego trips, busily mentally preparing for their turn to speak, they most likely won't be paying much attention to the person talking. So naturally the speaker will address himself to you. So will each of the others, in turn, when they speak.

By giving up the petty need to "tell others what you think", you will soon become central to the discussion without having said a word.

Listening with true interest will give you just as much enjoyment as speaking. You can laugh (to yourself) at what is going on, learn from it, obtain useful information

for your own purposes, whatever. Only if you sit there and "space out" will you feel, and be, left out. If you interact by looking at the speakers and conveying your interest with facial expression, your opinion will be sought after, and everyone will want you "on their side".

Instead of having to force your way into the conversation you will probably be asked to speak.

If you are . . .
(a) allow several seconds of silence before you begin
(b) speak softly, calmly and slowly
(c) say as little as possible.

Another interesting effect of speaking less is that people will want to "talk" with **you** and they will feel (correctly) that you are an excellent speaker.

Remember, you don't have to talk in order to have an opinion. The need to express your opinions to others is, most times, just a sign of weakness, ego or insecurity. It is impossible to say too little. It is very easy to say too much.

Even though you have as much "right" as the next person to speak, you don't have to exercise that right. You don't commit suicide just because you have as much "right" to as someone who did.

Everyone loves a listener.

Second Principle of Speaking:

avoid speaking expectations and judgments

On those occasions when you do decide to speak, avoid speaking words that simply represent your personal expectations or judgments.

At first it is probably best to say just about nothing for a week or so. During this period, you will notice several important things. First of all, you will realize that others are practically always just speaking their Expectations and Judgments. While they have a "right" to do this, you will realize that by endlessly babbling their opinions they are (most often) very boring to listen to and you will become careful not to tire others with tedious humdrum any more than you enjoy hearing it yourself. You will also probably want to start spending more time alone with yourself away from all the irrelevant noise and static.

Opinions can sometimes be less than fascinating.

Before you speak, consciously say to yourself, "Is what I am about to say an expectation or judgment? If it is, avoid it. NOTE: PRACTICALLY EVERYTHING WE SAY IS AN EXPECTATION OR JUDGMENT.

When we avoid speaking Expectations or Judgments, the number of words we speak should decrease by **90%** or more. At first it will be difficult to remember to consciously ask yourself if what you are about to speak is an Expectation or Judgment. You may think the whole idea is stupid and say to yourself, "Well, everything is an Expectation or Judgment, what am I supposed to do, never speak?" But learning how to apply this rule and in what manner, is the essence of the second Principle of Speaking.

Following this Principle is more difficult than following the First Principle (speak less).

Obviously, every human being is entitled to and has a wide variety of opinions and expectations on any number of endless subjects. Moreover, we all are equally entitled to express those opinions to others. HOWEVER, the mere fact that we are entitled to literally puff hot air out of our mouths in an attempt to get our share of opinions in, does not mean that expressing them is in our own best interest. Having an equal right with others to speak opinions doesn't necessarily make doing it a worthwhile endeavor.

Now if someone says "Would you like a piece of watermelon?" and you say "Yes", that is a judgment in some sense. So learning how to apply this second Principle of Speaking is a skill that must be developed by each of us.

You should, however, be aware that there are many things we can say that are absolutely not Expectations or Judgments. For example, we can say "thank you" or we can ask a question. Also, being asked by others to express our opinion is a valid use of speech **so long as we acknowledge that what we speak is just our opinion.**

Secondly, you will be pleased with yourself for not speaking this basically useless type of speech. Your energy will increase and you will begin to make exciting new observations as your consciousness and mental powers are no longer wasted on puffing out opinions. Silence will also tend to put the other "puffers" on the defensive, increasing your personal power that much more.

replace puffing out your expectations and judgments with the new perceptions and power of silence!

Third Principle of Speaking:

use the Power Speaking Techniques

don't be anxious to speak . . .

If we are sitting on the edge of our seat, or begin to speak practically before the other person has finished, our anxiety will be perceived by others either consciously or subconsciously. Wait for the "flow" to bring you a proper space for speaking. If it doesn't come you can live in silence. The best practical advice in this regard is: When you are about to speak allow a few seconds of silence before you begin. This has several advantages. It clears the air of the other speaker's vibrations; it allows and practically **commands attention** of others to be directed towards you; it conveys power and a sense of deliberation and wisdom.

speak softly and slowly . . .

The entire vibration of speaking softly and slowly is one of sharing instead of demanding. Speaking softly requires more concentration and attention from the listener. Speaking slowly adds greatly to the comprehension of, and impact on, the listener. Any of us would rather listen to a canary than a crow. By speaking softly and slowly it becomes difficult to project an angry or hostile emotion whatever the intellectual content of the words may be. Those who bluster and speak loudly, shrilly, or angrily, reveal weakness. Speaking softly and slowly displays and builds inner strength and confidence.

don't save face . . .

Look into the eyes of the people you are speaking with. If you are in a group discussion, alternate your eye contact. By not averting eye contact (although you may find it a little difficult or embarrassing at first), each person will appreciate it and want their "turn" from you.

Try to maintain the attitude of happiness and a smile in your being when you speak to others. Whether or not this reflects as a physical smile is not essential, but the vibration of happiness will show in your eyes and expression. **This definitely works.** For example, when singers are singing "flat" and they smile, their tones become on key.

Fourth Principle of Speaking:

exercise self control

of becoming angry, thereby throwing your sanity out the window, you can just as easily smile and say (to yourself only, if necessary), "Everyone is entitled to his own opinion." You will soon see that **by controlling the impulses of the body the only thing you are "losing" is unhappiness.** Having the right to argue isn't necessarily to our advantage. No one is "getting away" with anything on you; you are the one who is "getting away" with something—your peace and happiness—which you have consciously chosen not to throw away in idle opinion, arguments, or debates with others. When you so value your own happiness more than "proving yourself right", others will respect you more as well. If you are right, you have no need to prove it. Proving you are right is a definite drain of personal power. Remember, unless you exercise this control and avoid speaking in improper spaces, the mere intellectual understanding of the Principles of Speaking will be useless to you.

The first three Principles of Speaking (Speak Less, Avoid Expectation or Judgments, and the Power Speaking Techniques) are the physical and intellectual basis for making your words more valuable both to yourself and others as well as gaining new personal power and confidence.

The first three Principles of Speaking represent knowledge that you have been given. However, without the ability to exercise the will power of Self Control, this knowledge will only amount to cocktail party chatter.

Personal growth and expansion will come when you exercise the control over your Body to bypass a space that would have previously pulled you down to its level. For example, when someone says something that makes the body want to lash back—say you are falsely accused of something, whatever—instead of giving in to the impulse to attack, maintain control and say to yourself "That's not true—that's not me, it's just someone's opinion." Instead

The Four Principals
of Speaking

Chapter 5

THE EVERYTHING
YOU ALWAYS WANTED
CHAMBER OF HORRORS

What do you fear most?

POVERTY

CRITICISM

ILL HEALTH

LOST LOVE

OLD AGE

DEATH

Man has six basic fears. They are common to all of us and muddle up the best of psyches. These fears act as barriers and keep you from getting "Everything You Always Wanted." The rest of this book will show you how to rid yourself of these fears forever. Beyond that, the scope is unlimited. HOWEVER . . . reading this book will mean Nothing—Zero—unless you are willing to put at least some of the principles into active practice. So, if you TRULY desire to have "Everything You Always Wanted," read on in a spirit of adventure. If, on the other hand, you wish only to lose yourself in a few moments of entertainment to alleviate the pain of boredom, may we suggest a career in aviation.

For those of you who are still with us, here's . . .

Chapter 6

THE PERILOUS ADVENTURES
OF THE ELECTROMAGNETIC BODY

People are always asking others, "Do you believe in reincarnation?" Those people who want to believe in reincarnation generally do so because on some subconscious level they view it as a way of "getting out of dying". It's almost as if their ego says to itself, "Well, if I die, at least I'll be born again."

The "I" that most of us think we are, namely the body, cannot and (of course) does not survive when the body dies. The complete impossibility of our body surviving "death" is the reason that it is foolish to bet on the body and its temporary physical possessions. We know that such a bet always loses. All bodies crumble and die before the eyes of their occupants, so we have nothing to lose by "betting" on the permanence of our electromagnetic bodies since we know they last at least as long as the physical bodies, and even if we are skeptics, we must logically agree that it is at least possible that electromagnetic bodies last longer since no one has been able to prove otherwise.

As for bodies, history has proven they are always only temporary containers.

The body does not survive. So in that sense, there is no reincarnation. You should start accepting this fact now and prepare for it. Someday, the body must go! In fact, by tomorrow, it will be gone. The "You" that you call yourself tomorrow will be different by billions of atoms.

When the event of "death" occurs, the electromagnetic body which represents and contains our Intelligence, or consciousness, separates from the physical body.

The electromagnetic body, just like the physical body (and everything else in this Creation) has been and is undergoing continuous change during the entire lifetime of the human being in which it is centered.

The alterations and changes of the electromagnetic body are affected by the actions and experiences of the physical body in which it lives. Actions and experiences of the physical body affecting the electromagnetic body is a fact acknowledged by "modern science." For example, if we do not eat food for ten days, the presently measurable electromagnetic fields around the body will change.

Notice the subtle change in Fido's electromagnetic body after ten days without food.

Similarly, every action, thought and experience we have induces an alteration in the electromagnetic body. Whether or not some particular action or experience produces a presently "measurable" change is not important since what we can measure today depends only on the present state of technology which, like everything else, is always changing.

When we separate from our physical bodies, the electromagnetic body has recorded in it the cumulative effects of our entire lifetime.

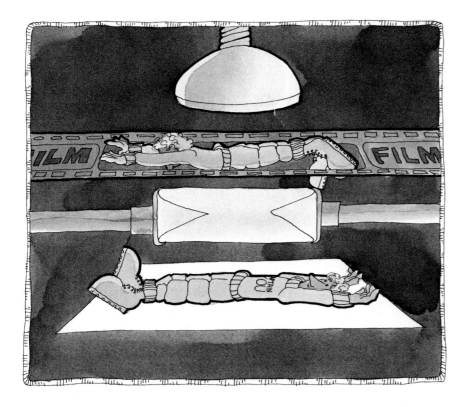

When light strikes a film negative, it leaves an impression on the light pattern of the negative. Similarly, when the energy of our actions, thoughts, and experiences strikes the "film" of the electromagnetic body, the electromagnetic body is altered.

So even though the electromagnetic body is free of the physical body after death (that is what death means) it has been permanently altered and affected by what took place during its life in the physical body.

The factors which determine what actions and experiences of the physical body cause which alterations in the electromagnetic body are called The Laws of The Cosmos.

Chapter 7

SOUP D'JOUR—
YOU ARE WHAT YOU EAT

the bod is sod . . .

Good nutrition is more than simply a matter of consuming alleged minimum daily requirements of certain chemical factors.

For example, this is not the way you should consume your minimum daily requirement of iron.

As material objects, our bodies are marvelously efficient and complex chemical factories. The elimination of waste matter and dead cells, the healing of wounds, the process of nourishing the live cells, all these are acts of the greatest intelligence. These things do not happen by chance. Some process of intelligence controls these actions.

The portion of our Intelligence controlling these involuntary, physiological functions is called the Instinctive Mind.

That which we call "intelligence" is usually connected with IQ tests, verbal argumentation, and college degrees. These are indeed levels of intelligence but by no means the only ones.

Some examples of intelligence.

90

Experimenski's Lemma . . .

The Intelligence which brought us into physical being will carry us through life—the power that took charge of us then has charge of us now and will have charge of us always.

To the extent that we open ourselves to the inflow of this great Intelligence we will be benefitted. If we fear it or choose to substitute words, doctors, theories, and placebos for the operation of the Instinctive Mind, we turn our backs on the very force that created and maintains our physical body.

The question is, "How do we get in touch with this great force in more than a verbal way?" First, we must respect it as true intelligence, although non-verbal. In order to develop this respect, we can actually speak to the Instinctive mind as though it was a separate being.

Studies undertaken by Nobel Prize winner, Igor Experimenski—the noted Siberian Parapsychologist discloses an effective method to contact the Instinctive Mind.

Quoting from Experimenski's lab experiment:
"Look at yourself in the mirror and say to your Instinctive Mind, Look here, ya, I know you don't understand vords and I don't understand the vay you voik, but I respect and tank you for doink your best, ya, overcomink my foolin avound an performink doas life-givink functions vithout vich I vould be dead. Schnookers, tank you and pliss keep up the good vork ya, because if you don't, then I heff to kiss strudel goodbye."

We have found that if you actually look at yourself and say these words (or others capturing the same essence) each day, then after a while in your consciousness there will begin to unfold the perception of another force at work within you in addition to your verbal Intellectual Mind.

CAUTION: Indiscriminate application of this technique produces a curious craving for Siberian pastries.

the vital force . . .

Health is the natural state of man. Disease is the absence of health. Disease is nothing more than that; disease.

We are so apt to consider and speak of Disease as an entity. We say that "it" attacks us, that "it" is very malignant, that "it" resists all treatment and so on. We speak of disease as if it were an entity with a character and disposition. We consider it as something that takes possession of us and uses its power for our destruction. We seek to kill it or at least scare it away. This perception is not the truth; we have not been attacked by some outside force. It is just that our body is out of balance and harmony because we have violated it. Doctors and drugs have an important place in the preservation of man's health and life in certain circumstances. But to live by lazy, abominable habits of sloth, be it improper eating or any other destructive pastimes and then taking refuge at the doctor's office when the situation gets obviously out of hand, is its own worst result.

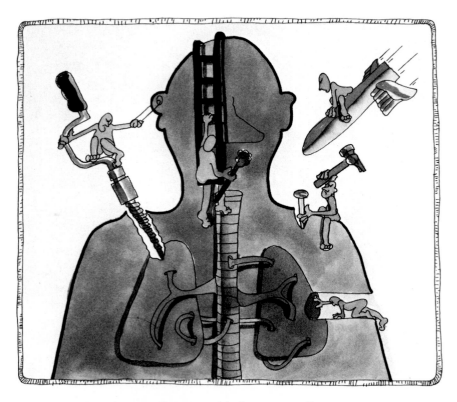

This is not disease, this is a scene from a television commercial

Nature usually gives us warnings before the onset of disease. Often the Instinctive Mind does such a good job despite the abuse we give it that the decay is gradual. Almost imperceptibly, we get fat and flabby, our energy begins to slip, the sparkle fades from our eyes and an ashen pallor replaces the pink glow of healthy cheeks. Like a person being slowly poisoned, we don't realize what is happening. The change of consciousness is so gradual, so imperceptible, it never seems like anything is going wrong. Beaten and dejected, we pick up a book called "Everything You Always Wanted" to find out what to do about this . . .

WHAT TO DO ABOUT THIS . . .

(1) Place the book on the floor face down.

(2) Unless you're looking up through a transparent floor (or have x-ray vision), you shouldn't be able to read this.

If we learn to feel the sensation of "hunger"—the physical signal for certain nutrients and learn to disregard "Bic Mac Attacks" and other artificial, phony "appetites" programmed into our Intellectual Mind by a profit-consumption oriented society, then we needn't follow a regimented program of limited intake known belovedly as "The Diet". However, we must exercise some control and this will not be easy at first because a body out of control will not yield willingly, any more than it yielded willingly to being toilet trained at the age of two.

We do not wish to be another nutritional "cookbook" and go on endlessly about "how many ounces of this" and "how many grams of that" you should eat in order to be eating naturally. However, here's general guidlines.

(a) **Stay close to nature**—raw fruits and vegetables, nuts, some cheeses, whole wheat breads, and juices represent the happiest food for the body. The closer what you consume is to its natural state, the better it is. (For example, eat raw carrots instead of cooked ones.) The above food categories, alone, provide more than enough nutrition and variety to support and nourish a beautiful body.

If you want to have a box of popcorn or something, don't hassle yourself. The basic long term habits are what will govern. Don't be "rule bound," but do consciously remember the guidelines.

(b) **Minimize consumption of animal flesh**—Animal flesh means any animal that had a nervous system. This includes meat, fish, birds, whatever. Hereafter, all these will be called "meat." Here's why meat should be avoided:

(i) Especially in America, most meat is raised under artifical "feed-lot" conditions. The animals are packed into tiny feed lots instead of grazing naturally on the open range. They are fed feed which has been grown of chemicals. Being highest on the food chain, the concentration of chemicals and toxins in the body of the animal—which is what you eat—is very high. They are force fed chemicals, some of which are known carcinogens, as well as weight enhancers designed to have them gain the most amount of weight possible before they are killed. Most of it is fat and water weight, but the growers get paid for it anyway. When the animals are led to slaughter they secrete adrenalin and other chemicals into their body tissue which adds to the chemicals, body toxins and poisons you consume.

(ii) Whenever you eat something you are saying in effect, "I choose to exchange my present body for the body that will result from the digestion and assimilation of this food." By eating meat you are choosing to exchange your present body for one that will have more of the vibration of dead, decaying flesh—which is all meat is—and adding all kinds of strange, dangerous toxins and poisons to your system. Your mental attitude and happiness are, of course, affected.

(iii) The idea that meat is necessary to the human diet as a source of protein is a complete hype. Nature provides us with superior foods—some providing pound for pound five to ten times more protein than meat.

(c) **Avoid junk food**—Junk food consists of most things sold in American supermarkets—sugar, cookies, soda-pop, frozen dinners and most cereals. All so-called "fast food" items are in this category. It should really be called "fast-buck" food. What you are really buying and trying to bite into is an appealing psychological image which you have been subliminally sold. In most cases you would be better off fasting than eating these. Also included in this category are most canned and pre-cooked foods. Most canned and pre-cooked foods are devoid of the enzymes necessary for good digestion. Without the proper enzymes, your body cannot even process the food properly.

(d) **Minimize use of drugs**—Tobacco, alcohol, marijuana, speed, "uppers," "downers," whatever, all are food. They are ingested and merge with and become the body, which is what food means. They have little or no nutritive value and all are literally poison to the system. In fact, they achieve their effect by poisoning the system in various ways. We call this "getting high" because the cumulative effect of our past bad habits has made us so dulled out and sluggish that any "sensation" feels good.

(e) **Drink plenty of water**—Drink as many glasses of water a day as you can. Drink frequently, but do not drink too much at once. Water irrigates and washes the entire internal body. It provides a basic ingredient of blood, it keeps the bowels moving and irrigated. Constipation is a major cause of disease as the toxins that should be eliminated fester within the body and feed back into the system and this, of course, is not "Everything You Always Wanted."

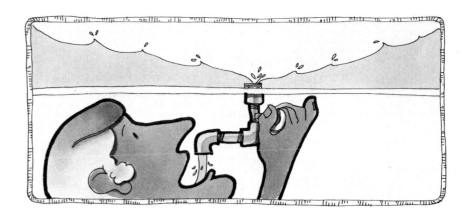

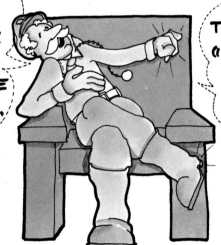

—by General Guidelines

further comments on food . . .

1. EAT LESS

In most cases, the physical volume of food we consume is excessive. This results from several possible causes including the fact that eating is often a psychological security blanket or a psychological satisfaction (these attitudes are fostered by the advertising system) having nothing to do with the nutritive needs of our body and the stomach is simply the place where that which has been eaten ends up.

Another cause of excessive eating is impaired or inefficient bodily functions. If our past habits have caused our digestive system and colon to become clogged with mucus, slime and other residue, the digestive assimulation is impaired and in order to meet our nutritive requirements we may need to eat three or four times the normal volume of food. This is a vicious cycle because if our digestion and assimilation is inefficient we have to eat much more to get the same results. But this excessive eating puts even more of a load on the system to process food and produces further excessive waste matter the body cannot eliminate.

The only way to break the cycle is to stop eating as much. It is better to be a little hungry than to stuff the body. When your body gets healthier, it will not enjoy, nor will it be necessary to tolerate, any of the things it does presently.

2. CHEW BABY, CHEW

While you're eating, take time to chew your food. If we chew our food until it is broken up into a fine paste we aid the assimilation of the food into the body. The salivary enzymes that mix with food form an important part of the ingredients necessary for digestion. By chewing slowly and thoroughly we also break the food into smaller particles, exposing more of the food to digestive juices in the stomach. By bolting our food down, we only exhibit an impulsive instinct and give the stomach a mass of putrifying matter which becomes a burden—slowing you down, keeping you from getting "Everything You Always Wanted."

Chapter 8

WONDERFUL ENERGY

We'd like to take this time out

to tell you about

100

As you may recall, everything is made of energy. Wonderful Energy is the name we give to the pool of primal force behind this creation, the sum total of all energy. From now on we will refer to this as 𝖂𝕰. Unlike the Individual Intelligences (electromagnetic bodies) and other aspects of nature as manifested on the physical plane 𝖂𝕰 are constant and unchanging. 𝖂𝕰 cannot be described in words because 𝖂𝕰 are more than words. A part of something cannot describe the whole of it.

A part of something cannot describe the whole of it.

𝖂𝕰 are the creator of all thoughts, words, ideas, objects; in fact all manifestations of creation because 𝖂𝕰 are beyond the limits of time and space. 𝖂𝕰 are the "white light" of this universe. Just as all the colors of the rainbow are inherent in white light, all the things, ideas, and manifestations of the physical universe are inherent in 𝖂𝕰.

Trying to logically understand 𝖂𝕰 is like one of the rays of the rainbow trying to comprehend the white light from which the entire rainbow manifests. Similarly, all objects, people, ideas, and thoughts are only just "rays" of the rainbow of creation which emanates from 𝖂𝕰.

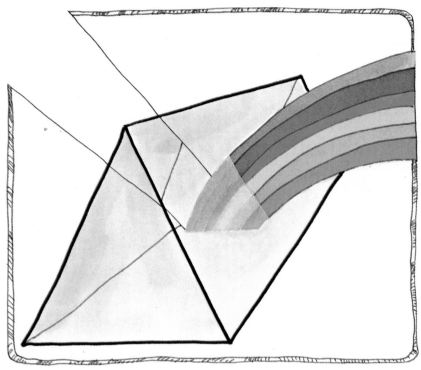

Each time the prism is tilted at a slightly different angle, a slightly different rainbow, or manifestation, appears.

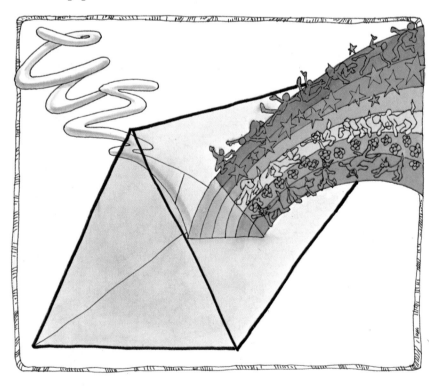

If we stand on the rainbow side of the prism, all we see are the infinite twinkling rays of the rainbow. We do not doubt that the white light exists just because we can't point to it. We understand that the white light is the source from which each of the rays of the rainbow originates. Although not itself directly visible, we understand that the white light permeates each and every one of the rainbow colors.

We say that things like stars, dogs, people and planets exist because they seem to on the earth plane, but do they really?

Choose one:
- ☐ **this is Noah's Ark**
- ☐ **this is the earth plane**
- ☐ **this is TWA's night coach to Cincinnati**

Look back on your own life ten years ago to the things that seemed important to you on the earth plane. Compared to now, probably many of the things seem meaningless, and so it is with all temporary manifestations (which includes everything) on the physical plane. They come and go like fleeting rainbows.

Although 𝔚𝔈 cannot be "pointed to", it permeates each and every one of its manifestations (e.g., plants, dogs, stars, people) or "rays", just like the white light permeates each color of the rainbow. This is what we mean when we say that 𝔚𝔈 is "omnipresent". Each and every thing in the Universe is no more or less than a "ray" of the "rainbow" of creation refracted through the "prism" of nature from 𝔚𝔈, the constant unchanging source of energy in the universe.

The "prism" of nature is in eternal ceaseless motion. This motion results in ever-changing "rays" or manifestations on the physical plane. This is why change and growth, birth and death, are inevitable. By recognizing our true position as "rays" in the rainbow of creation, we realize that 𝔚𝔈 are the true power of creation and therefore the fleeting rainbow images no longer have the power to affect our lives. We are the control.

Some of you might be bothered by the previous discussion.

Tough dudy.

That doesn't change the reality of the situation.

re·al·i·ty (rĭ al′e tĭ), *n.,*
that which happens most of the time

mir·a·cle (mĭr′e kel), *n.,*
that which happens infrequently

For example, a rock falls to earth when dropped

104

We in the western world are caught in the sparkle of science and technology and the egotistical assumption that unless something can be "explained" by science, it cannot be. Whether science can explain something has only to do with the present state of intellect and instruments. The fact that science cannot explain something does not negate its existence. Heaven forbid if science should say you don't exist!

All our fears stem from an incorrect identification of ourselves with the physical body. This results from a lack of knowledge of our true nature.

Pursuing only these temporary sense satisfactions will not yield permanent happiness. Seeking only the temporary pleasure of the senses is as useless and hopeless as putting on fresh make-up while your jetliner is going down in flames.

When a man dies, his family and friends gather around him.
They may even accompany him to the burial ground.

But not one of his friends or relatives is prepared to go with him.

There is only one "friend" who accompanies the dead man. It's 𝔚𝔈

Knowing that 𝔚𝔈 is your own inner reality provides da greatest wealth and satisfaction . . . total freedom and power forever. That is,

everything you always wanted

THE EYAW CROSSWORD PUZZLE

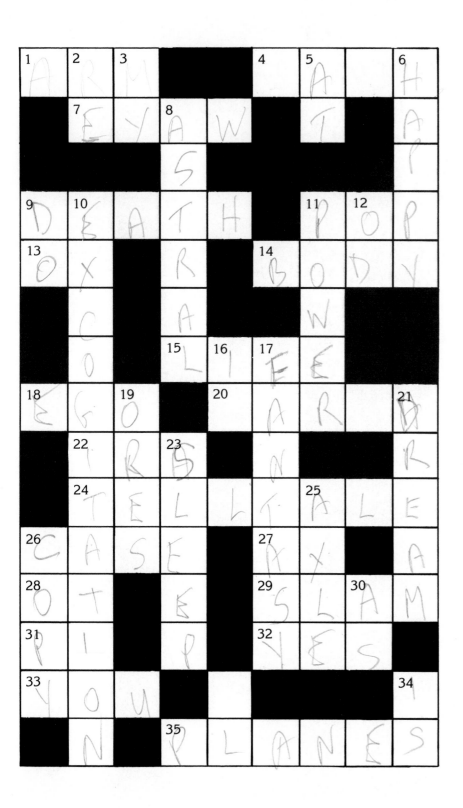

ACROSS

1. This is attached to your shoulder
4. Sometimes found in a garden
7. What we sometimes call this book in order to save trees
9. This cannot happen to your electromagnetic body
11. Soda or dad
13. This can very stubborn
14. You have two, one physical & one electromagnetic
15. Neither Time nor Newsweek
18. Watch out if yours gets too big
20. A measure of electric capacitance
22. Who you pay every April 15
24. Don't let your tongue be this
26. Check a place before a burglary
27. To fire: colloq.
28. Abbreviation for overtime
29. Grand _____
31. Ratio of the circumference of a circle to its diameter
32. Affirmative response
33. A character in EYAW
35. Astral & Earth are examples of these

DOWN

2. Legal abbreviation meaning regarding
3. Possessive
5. "where it's _____"
6. What you should be after reading EYAW
8. The plane you go to after life
9. Sounds like "dew"
10. For this you get a penny
11. EYAW can help develop yours
12. This happens if you mess with drugs
16. This stood stiff
17. A mental imagining
19. Metals often come from these
21. Life is no more than this
23. We do this at night
25. Connects the wheels of your car
26. Imitate
30. "_____ you like it"
34. Exists

Chapter 9

THE PLANES OF LIFE

Thousands of radio vibrations may permeate and interpenetrate each other in a given city. With the aid of a tuner and our ears we can hear any station.

Similarly, there might be fourteen worlds occupying the same portions of space, each one on a far different vibratory frequency and yet none interfering with the others—the living things on each plane being as unaware of the existence of those of the other as radio waves occupying the same portion of physical space are of each other. By expanding our minds beyond the physical plane, we can become sensitive to these other levels of existence.

Just because we only see one color of the rainbow, does not mean that it is the only color that exists. Just because we tune in to one radio station it does not mean others are not broadcasting.

Similarly, just because we can see only the tangible "reality" before us, does not preclude the reality of other levels of existence. In fact, by expanding our minds beyond the physical plane, we can become sensitive to many other levels of being previously undreamed of.

L. TRYON-TATOIAN

a word on science . . .

Journal of Nuclear Hypocrisy
Vol LXVII   *Issue 18*

In our technologically oriented Western civilization legitimacy is often withheld from an area of inquiry until it has received the imprimatur of science. In our justifiable admiration and respect for science we must remember one basic fact: everything that science "knows" or claims to be true is dependent on the present state of technology and is always changing. Whether present-day scientific technology can measure or "prove" the existence of something has nothing to do with whether or not that thing is possible, or whether it exists.

Science used to think we couldn't fly in airplanes; science used to think the world was flat. Unless some scientist cares to come forth and claim the present state of knowledge represents the absolute truth and that there will be no new knowledge, or progress, or discoveries, then whether present-day science agrees or disagrees with the axioms of integrated electromagnetic calculus, or can "prove" them is totally irrelevant.

Similar to the uproar caused by the discovery of the earth's heliocentric revolution, five hundred years from now "modern scientists" will sit back and laugh; "Imagine", they will say, "in the late 1970s the instrumentation and techniques were so crude they could barely even measure or detect the electromagnetic body."

Consider the following example.

Normally, if we can see and feel an object with our senses, we call it real. However, it is also common knowledge that the senses are fallible and what we see and feel may not be what really exists. For instance, the senses tell us that the surface of this paper is smooth and clean, but if it is observed through a powerful microscope, it will be found to be covered with fine dust and other particles.

Journal of Nuclear Hypocrisy
Vol LXVII   *Issue 18*

Still, the whole truth is not known about this surface, because if a scanning electron microscope were to be focused on this apparently clean surface, then we would gather even more information than before, which could not be seen with the ordinary microscope.

This is an endless process. With every technological advance, we open a new door and find ten more doors which still remain unopened. Thus, no matter at what stage of the investigation we assess our information, it is always bound to be incomplete and relative, and never the absolute Truth.

Science is a wonderful fool, but the danger lies in the assumption that what is presently thought to be reality is the absolute truth. This is, of course, not so.

All scientific knowledge is relative.

There is always a deeper level of observation, new theories and new explanations. Scientific knowledge exists as a function of time; it is never absolute.

Fig Newton

Astral planes are levels of immeasurably high vibrational frequencies that give rise to the psychic activities known as clairvoyance, telepathy, psychokinesis and similar other "ESP" phenomena.

Although our vibratory rate and hence our perceptive capabilities are largely centered in the material world, the border between the material and Astral planes is continuous, not discrete, and can therefore be consciously transversed. Rather as a person with unusually keen hearing whose ears hear frequencies much higher than most people, certain of us have the capabilities to perceive vibratory planes higher than the material ones most of us are presently limited to. These people are then said to possess "Extra-Sensory Perceptive Abilities".

Astral Flights in the dream state (to be discussed) represent the projection of our consciousness from the material world, where it is usually centered, into the higher more subtle vibratory planes. These Astral projections can occur during sleep and also in certain trance-like states; in Pennsylvania and Arkansas, for example.

Chapter 10

EXCOGITATION: A PENNY FOR YOUR THOUGHTS

Excogitation is the process by which the electromagnetic body manifests itself upon the earth plane through the material brain and sensory organs.

Every impulse emanating from the Electromagnetic Body and vibrating through the material brain produces a manifestation known on this earth plane as thought. An ordinary sequence of these thoughts constitutes the process we call Thinking. While living on the physical plane, the Electromagnetic Body manifests itself primarily through the physical brain.

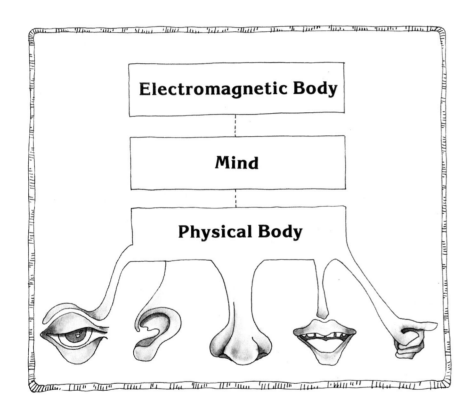

It is in the process of thinking that we superimpose our material expectations, assumptions and beliefs. It is on this level that we get tricked into believing we are only the body; causing us tremendous anxiety, grief, frustration, dilemmas, turmoil and all other unnecessary hassles.

The mind is the connection between the physical and electromagnetic body. In actuality, the mind is just a prism that reflects the vibrations of the electromagnetic body into the experiences and perceptions that we call the "real world."

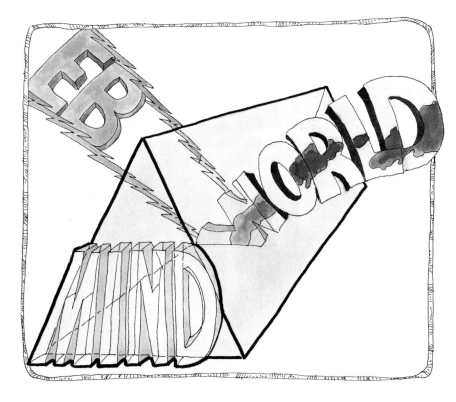

The electromagnetic body as seen through the prism of the mind is the physical world.

At this point you're probably wondering where this prism is located. It's sitting on the dining room table in Sylvia Goldberg's condominium, 5522 Collins Avenue, Miami Beach, Florida.

If we can stop thought even for a moment, we will establish a direct link between ourselves as the physical body and ourselves as the Electromagnetic Body.

WE SHALL CALL STOPPING ALL THOUGHT "STOPPING THE WORLD"

When we succeed at truly Stopping The World, our physical bodies contact our electromagnetic bodies directly without the intermediary of the mind. This produces an energizing sensation in the physical body that is truly indescribable to those who have not personally experienced it. When we achieve the surge of perfection and energy that comes with Stopping The World, we get in touch with true peace and happiness. When we Stop The World a surge of incredible energy pulses through our being and if we can control it, the energy surges right out past the physical confines of our bodies. When this happens, we **know** (not think) that the Electromagnetic Body is timeless and exists independent of the physical body. Being able to contact and feel this sensation proves to all those who experience it that we are more than the body and that the Electromagnetic Body can never die. We thereby **know that the real us is immortal.**

The ideas and procedures set forth in EYAW are designed to help you "train" for the "big event" of Stopping the World. It is not an easy task, and many may be tempted to give up from impatience and despair before reaching the goal. However, this is the only game in town.

Two of our previous EYAW users, training for the big event.

Chapter 11

HUMILITY IS NEVER HAVING TO SAY YOU'RE SORRY

don't believe your I's . . .

It is through the use of the physical body that the electromagnetic body acquires a knowledge and experience of phenomena upon this physical plane of life.

Through personal experience acquired via the physical body and the exercise of reason and intuition, the electromagnetic body discovers, to some degree or another, the existence of Nature's laws and its relationship to those laws.

The totality of the laws of the Cosmos exist, independent of the existence or perception of any person. The totality of these laws is what we mean by TRUTH. No physical body is "perfect", so its sensory perceptions will be something less than 100% of TRUTH as it applies to the physical plane of existence.

The result is that for each of us the Totality of the Laws of the Cosmos (TRUTH) is filtered through the physical body. The net result is the filtered perception of each person, that which we call "opinions". Many of us have not really stopped to realize that what we think to be "reality" is, in TRUTH, only a filtered perception. Because the body tends to be a self-centered entity, few of us have developed the humility to accept our perceptions as only a filtered refraction of the TRUTH. **Accepting this fact is what we mean by humility.** The reason why being humble is so much in our own self-interest is that by being humble, we can accept that our perceptions are only our individual interpretations, not reality. This is a prerequisite of searching for an expanded view of TRUTH; and the more expanded our perceptions become, the happier and healthier we will be because we will be more in harmony with the laws of the Cosmos.

Humility is an asset you can bank on.

125

false notions of humility . . .

Being humble (accepting the fact that our beliefs are only that which we "see" through the colored window panes of the mind and the physical body) is more than something to say at Sunday School. Without humility it is impossible to broaden the horizons of our perceptions because to some degree or another we are attached and clinging to the false notion that what we presently believe is, in fact, true.

Being humble does not mean letting others take advantage of you.

This is not humility, this is a scene from Kojak.

It means accepting the fact that another person's filtered perceptions and beliefs deserve as much respect and consideration as your own.

Sometimes our preconceptions cause errors in judgment.

Living in a state of tolerance (versus merely mouthing the words at parties and PTA meetings) has many practical advantages for every individual.

For example if a bird cockies in your face, don't get angry, simply shoot it.

So, instead of getting into a fight with someone and becoming angry, hateful, frustrated, and unhappy, you can look at the space and say "Oh well, I guess his filters are just different from mine."

"Oh, well, I guess his filters are just different from mine."

This is how the Cosmos works; by giving you receive—the giving and receiving goes beyond the material. By being humble you are better off, happier, because you bypass negative spaces; and the world is better off because you aren't putting angry, negative vibrations into the air.

Just like playing tennis, humility is a practical, working skill that can be developed by practice and the exercise of Will. Knowing the words is not enough, we must put it to practical use every day. Even when the other person is being outrageous, we must exercise the discipline and willpower to be humble so we can bypass the space and be happy instead of being unhappy. If someone is an arrogant jerk, we can't change it. We can only choose to let ourselves get involved, thereby choosing to be unhappy, or we can choose to be "humble" and happy. Which would you rather be?

Chapter 12

REINCARNATION:
THE OPPORTUNITY OF A LIFETIME

Words, actions and thoughts that are in accordance with constructive forces produce constructive reactions; words, actions and thoughts that are in accordance with destructive forces produce destructive reactions.

Waves of a feather flock together.

The way this happens is as follows: When an electromagnetic body is acted upon by either a constructive force or a destructive force, the electromagnetic body undergoes an electromagnetic alteration corresponding to the nature of the force which acted upon it. If an electromagnetic body contains the cumulative imprint of many destructive forces, it will attract from the Cosmos other electromagnetic bodies and forces which have been similarly altered.

Conversely, if an electromagnetic body contains the cumulative imprint of many constructive forces, it will attract similarly constructively altered electromagnetic bodies to it.

By affecting the type of electromagnetic bodies and forces we attract utilizing either constructive or destructive forces, we always ensure that we attract, at some point in our future evolution, exactly those types of reactions that we initially projected out into the universe. **We are not punished or rewarded for our actions, but by them.**

Because the law of Action/Reaction does not always equal out in the short run, and because the body is like a dope addict who wants to be satisfied at all costs, we may lose sight of the inevitable applicability of this law.

I can't get no satisfaction.

As you may remember from our previous discussion of the Astral planes, there are levels of vibration beyond the physical plane. For example, there's the Great Planes, the not-so-great planes, and the Plain Jane's.

Kom Plane, the irate Norwegian carpenter and hobby scientist, discovered while flying his Cessna 600 from Hammerfest to Konskie, Poland, the connection between all of the planes. This fundamental truth which rests at the cornerstone of modern theoretical physics is known as Kom Plane's Law (not to be confused with Kom Plane's in-laws).

Kom Plane's In-Laws

This staggering law, which shook the very foundations of modern theoretical physics, and has been compared in impact with Einstein's theory of relativity, expresses . . .

the connection

between   the   planes . . .

The following equations are mathematical statements of Kom Plane's Law in three and four dimensional space.

Three dimensions

$$\boldsymbol{A} = (A_x, A_y, A_z)$$

$$\boldsymbol{A} \cdot \boldsymbol{B} = A_x B_x + A_y B_y + A_z B_z$$

$$\boldsymbol{\nabla} = (\partial/\partial x, \partial/\partial y, \partial/\partial z)$$

$$\nabla \psi = \left(\frac{\partial \psi}{\partial x}, \frac{\partial \psi}{\partial y}, \frac{\partial \psi}{\partial z} \right)$$

$$\boldsymbol{\nabla} \cdot \boldsymbol{A} = \frac{\partial A_x}{\partial x} + \frac{\partial A_y}{\partial y} + \frac{\partial A_z}{\partial z}$$

$$\boldsymbol{\nabla} \cdot \boldsymbol{\nabla} = \frac{\partial^2}{\partial x^2} + \frac{\partial^2}{\partial y^2} + \frac{\partial^2}{\partial z^2}$$

Four dimensions

$$a_\mu = (a_t, a_x, a_y, a_z) = (a_t, \boldsymbol{a})$$

$$a_\mu b_\mu = a_t b_t - a_x b_x - a_y b_y - a_z b_z = a_t b_t - \boldsymbol{a} \cdot \boldsymbol{b}$$

$$\nabla_\mu \, (\partial/\partial t, \, -\partial/\partial x, \, -\partial/\partial y, \, -\partial/\partial z) = (\partial/\partial t, \, -\boldsymbol{\nabla})$$

$$\nabla_\mu \varphi = \left(\frac{\partial \varphi}{\partial t}, \, -\frac{\partial \varphi}{\partial x}, \, -\frac{\partial \varphi}{\partial y}, \, -\frac{\partial \varphi}{\partial z} \right) = \left(\frac{\partial \varphi}{\partial t}, \, \boldsymbol{\nabla}\varphi \right)$$

$$\nabla_\mu a_\mu = \frac{\partial a_t}{\partial t} + \frac{\partial a_x}{\partial x} + \frac{\partial a_y}{\partial y} + \frac{\partial a_z}{\partial z} = \frac{\partial a_t}{\partial t} + \boldsymbol{\nabla} \cdot \boldsymbol{a}$$

$$\nabla_\mu \nabla_\mu = \frac{\partial^2}{\partial t^2} - \frac{\partial^2}{\partial x^2} - \frac{\partial^2}{\partial y^2} - \frac{\partial^2}{\partial z^2} = \frac{\partial^2}{\partial t^2} - \nabla^2 = \square^2$$

Upon "death" (sometimes referred to as "transition"), the Electromagnetic Body enters a new life upon the astral plane. This means that when the electromagnetic body separates from the physical body you no longer exist on this material level of consciousness; rather, you exist on an altogether different vibratory frequency and those frequencies of consciousness are what the astral planes are.

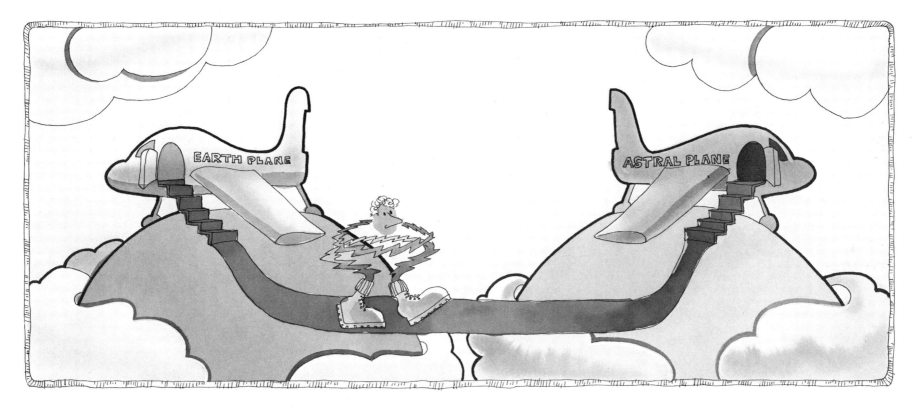

Death is nothing more than the transition of the electromagnetic body from one plane to the next.

No matter how great life is on the Astral Plane, the least little desire for things available only on the earth inevitably leads to another rebirth.

**The electromagnetic body falls into a current
sweeping it towards rebirth.**

Reaching the shores of life, each electromagnetic body chooses its destination.

In its new incarnation, each electromagnetic body goes to where it belongs by reason of what it is.

The Shores of Life

In its new incarnation, each electromagnetic body goes to where it belongs by reason of what it is.

It is not subject to the arbitrary dictates of any being in heaven or earth. Rather, the absolutely just and fair law of Action/Reaction applies. **Desire determines destiny.**

There is no favoritism, nor the slightest chance of any injustice being the fate of any electromagnetic body, no matter how lowly or humble it may be. Desire, not reward or punishment by some external force, is the motive power for our rebirth and the circumstances thereof.

To some, it may seem as if rebirth on the earth is something that is forced upon the electromagnetic body despite its wish to "be in heaven"; that is, on the astral Planes.

The very opposite is true, for the sum of the desires of the electromagnetic body constitutes the actual motive power leading to rebirth; which simply means a shift in the vibratory level upon which the electromagnetic body desires to exist.

Those electromagnetic bodies that are reborn upon the earth are not reborn against their will or desire. On the contrary, they are reborn because they actually desire it. They are carried into the current of rebirth because their desires and tastes have created longings that can be satisfied only by renewed life in the flesh.

When the level of vibration of the energy of the electromagnetic body changes frequency, the electromagnetic body changes its state of consciousness—perhaps now tuning in on that "frequency" which represents this material plane of existence. Instead of going to the movies, reincarnation represents being born into one. **Remembering that we are living a dream is the secret of obtaining peace and happiness.**

Although they are not conscious of it, they instinctively place themselves again within the operation of the Law of Action/Reaction and are swept onto rebirth in the environment best calculated to help them live out, express and exhaust the force of their desires. They hunger to satisfy their longings and until that hunger is appeased, the desires cannot be discarded. This does not mean that every desire must necessarily be lived out, for it happens frequently that a new insight or experience causes the electromagnetic body to turn with loathing from the former object of desire, and the desire is bypassed. But so long as the desire remains alive, it tends to attract the electromagnetic body towards objects and environments that seem likely to satisfy it.

Don't ask that any more!

Becoming aware of the other levels of exis-tence will give you more power than you ever imagined possible on earth plane.

Becoming aware of the other levels of existence will enable you to travel in an instant to far-off places.

Becoming aware of the other levels of existence will make you the Supreme master of any situation.

Becoming aware of the other levels of existence will enable you to face the IRS without guilt.

Escape from the earth to greater levels of power is possible when the Electromagnetic Body learns the TRUTH regarding Creation. Then, the ties of the material world begin to slip away. When the true nature of earthly things is realized, they lose their hold on the Electromagnetic Body. Desire then dies away and the Electromagnetic Body rises to infinite heights of power!

149

now isn't that

**everything you
always wanted**

Chapter 13

LIFE IS BUT A DREAM

Row, row, row your boat
gently down the stream.
Merrily, merrily, merrily,
merrily, life is but a dream.
— Anonymous

We'd like to take this second time out

to thank Anonymous, who wrote so many
pertinent enlightening and enriching ditties.

what is a dream?

and what is reality?

**understanding
the preceding
illustrations will
give you . . .**

everything you always wanted

Our bodies try to laugh and say that "Of course being awake is more "real" than "dreaming". But is this true?

The assertion that the waking state is "real" and the dream state is "just a dream" comes from our Body, a lower level in the order of the Cosmos. The only thing that differs between the Waking State and the Dream State is the conscious perception of the five senses (the physical embodiment of the Ego) which is turned on during the Waking State. It is this very Body-Ego that is making the claim that its conscious existence is the *sine qua non* of reality. It is like a spoiled brat saying "If I'm not awake there is no 'reality'." As we can see, **five body senses awake or five body senses asleep does not make for more or less reality.** Our electromagnetic bodies, our true essence are equally existent whether the body senses are "on" or "off".

Remember that the only difference between the Waking State and the Dream State is that the five physical senses are on or off respectively.

That which interprets the data of the five senses, the true perceptor of reality is always on.

When the Body-Ego gets turned off it tries to tell us "this isn't real". To give the body senses such control is to become a slave to a lump of flesh.

Giving up complete control to the body senses is being a slave to a lump of flesh.

dream \ ˈdrēm\ *n. often attrib* [ME *dreem,* fr. OE *drēam* noise, joy]: that which appears to be real and permanent in our consciousness at one point in time and not there at another.

Both the Waking State and Dream State qualify as "dreams". During our "day-dreams", that which seemed real and there during our "night dreams" is not there, and during our "night-dreams" that which seemed real and there during our "day-dreams" is not there.

But you may say, "Wait, there is a difference. When I go to sleep, I cannot, by exercise of my will, go back to some certain place or contact some certain person in the Dream State, whereas I can go back to some certain location or contact some certain person by exercise of choice in the Waking State."

While this difference presently does indeed exist be-between these two states for most of us, it is due to two factors:

(a) The structure and nature of the five physical Ego-Body senses, and

(b) Our inability, due to lack of training and technique, to exercise conscious control in the Dream State—which, in reality (HA, HA, HA) can be done!

Both of these factors are only limitations of the mind and body perceptions and do not affect the basic underlying equality of the Waking State and the Dream State.

With respect to giving greater value to the Waking State because we can go to people and places by will; this occurs only because the world of material objects and the five physical senses is vibrationally "slower" than the world of energy and consciousness that exists beyond the material senses. **Therefore, material spaces change more slowly, though just as inexorably,** so that when we "go back" to spaces, they are still there.

For example, in the material world if we want to go from Los Angeles to New York, this cannot be done instantaneously. We must make a reservation, drive to the airport, hassle luggage and lines, and sit on an airplane for five hours. All these actions are preceded by thought. Nothing happens on this earth without being preceded by a thought, because matter (the things on the earth) is inherently passive, that is, it is acted upon by Intelligence. So once we have the thought, it takes time and energy for the thought to manifest on the physical plane. The Dream State is like a well edited movie: we get on the plane in Los Angeles and "cut to" the plane landing in New York; all the slow, heavy, boring things are eliminated.

The clearer and more powerful our mind, the less attached we are to the body; and the more we are in touch with "We," the faster we can materialize our various thoughts on the earth plane.

The world of the dream state is no less "real" than the material state. It is simply not bound by the "slow", "heavy" laws of physical time and space. For example, in the dream state it may take only a thought and an instant to go from Los Angeles to New York. You may say, "But that wasn't real. I didn't go to New York. I only dreamed I was there." But when you "actually" go to New York what more do you have when you return than the same mental recollection of having been there? Once the event is past, saying "I dreamed I was in New York" or "I was in New York" are the same; they are both descriptions of your perception of events in the past. They have both come and gone—neither presently exist, or ever will again.

"Oh", you may say. "But in 'reality' (the Waking State) I can do things that help me get what I want. A dream is just something in my mind, I can't make any 'progress' in getting the things I want in dreams."

This is not so, however. First of all, as our mind and body become clearer and more powerful, the dreams we have, which are then called "astral flights" become important tools in helping us to decide matters pertaining to the Waking State. Even in our presently polluted bodies and untrained minds, we occasionally "get the answer" to a "problem" in a "dream".

Secondly, if we believe that we can actually get that which we desire only in the Waking State, we should ask ourselves the question, "What is it that we want?" What we want may seem permanent and necessary now, but stop to think about it for a moment.

When you were two years old, "that which you wanted" in your then "true waking state" which you couldn't make progress towards getting in "dreams" was a baby rattle. You don't even want that now. Do you? So what did it matter? In fact, you were better off sleeping in peace than crying and screaming because your two-year-old senses couldn't have the satisfaction of its then desire in "true reality."

But you say, "Oh, I was just a baby. Things are different now." Think of the desire for romance and sex that exists in a person of thirty. That's no child, that's a real desire we all identify with. But ask a man or woman of 65 years of age, and they say "Ah, yes, back in those days that stuff really mattered, but now I hardly remember, I just like to play golf and sit in the sun."

Stop a moment, look around you at what is called "reality." What do you see before you that will be here in ten years . . . a hundred years . . . a thousand years?

The truth of the matter is that regardless of the time it takes to disappear, nothing on the physical plane will last.

WHAT DOES THIS MEAN?

It means that

When the level of vibration of the energy of the electromagnetic body changes frequency, the electromagnetic body changes its state of consciousness—perhaps now tuning in on that "frequency" which represents this material plane of existence. Instead of going to the movies, reincarnation represents being born into one. **Remembering that we are living a dream is the secret of obtaining peace and happiness.**

By gaining control of ourselves on the Astral Planes, **WE** will be able to bridge gaps in time and space.

WE WILL BECOME...

THE BADDEST MUTHA IN TOWN

Here's "You" arguing with the arrogant jerk teller.

Arguing becomes unnecessary.

EYAW SCRAMBLEGRAM

INSTRUCTIONS:

1. Take each word and unscramble it.
2. Write it, one letter per box in the boxes next to each word.
3. Take all the circled letters and unscramble them to complete the quote at the bottom of the page.
4. Clue for quote: "Everything you'll ever need to know about Creation".

TERBTU

ITDYE

NEFSRID

MEBAL

NIDAME

QUOTE

Chapter 14

ASTRAL POWER TECHNIQUES

As physically embodied human beings we probably spend more time in sleeping than on any other single activity in our lives. Yet most of us waste these precious hours that we could be investing in our future happiness and prosperity.

WHAT IS SLEEP?

Sleep is when the physical body and the material cells comprising the brain are supposed to rest. Sleep requirements of about six or seven hours a day are typical. Requirements in excess of this amount can stem from a variety of causes, including:

(a) Boredom
(b) Need to "escape" from something
(c) Wasting energy by speaking too much or too loudly
(d) Wasting energy by breathing improperly
(e) Internal body pollution which leads to disease and cancer and requires the body to work overtime
(f) Overweight which causes the body to have to work unnecessarily

PRE-SLEEP ACTIVITIES

What we do and think in the hours before we go to sleep has a significant impact on the quality of our sleep and the quantity of sleep that we require.

Anything that excites the mind or body immediately before or during sleep will decrease its replenishing value. For example, if we eat a big "midnight snack" before going to sleep our bloodstream and digestive tract must work all night instead of restoring itself, and centers in the brain must remain alert to direct the activity. This is so simple and obvious that many of us "forget it." We would rather pretend that we are pursuing health and peace by taking a vitamin pill or buying junk food that says "Enriched with Vitamin C" than change old, comfortable habits of the Body. But remember that satisfying the senses often uses Destructive Forces and these forces work against the very body that is using them to seek its satisfaction. To gain more power during your sleep, follow our Major Rules.

our Major Rules

why do we have nightmares...

Nightmares are expressions of fears. These fears result from lack of knowledge of our true selves. It is a Destructive Process and results in nervous disorganization and disintegration. Negative eating patterns and attitudes contribute to nightmares.

Nightmares without fear are impossible.

effects of drugs on sleep . . .

Whether it's a beer, a shot of whiskey, a joint of mari-juana, or a sleeping pill makes no difference; the effect on quality of sleep is obviously negative. To tell ourselves otherwise is a complete lie and a drain on our personal power. If we still desire to do it, we should be realistic about the effect.

Requiring drugs to go to sleep stems from excessive bondage to and lack of control over the senses, which are in such rampant control that they literally have to be chemically knocked out. You drug the senses because you want to control them and make them stop, but you can't do it on your own.

**Some of us are in the habit of
occasionally using drugs to help us unwind.**

REGULARLY USING DRUGS IN CONNEC-
TION WITH GOING TO SLEEP IS TOTAL
PROOF THAT YOU ARE UNABLE TO CON-
TROL YOUR BODY AND YOUR SENSES.

You may or may not be able to regain control depending on your willpower and character. When we need drugs to help with sleep, it means that the Ego is so scared and attacked it is literally fighting not to lose control even to go to sleep, even though sleep would help it. This is just another example of how allowing the Body-Ego to seek its own satisfactions ends up destroying the Body itself.

Physically speaking, drugged sleep is unhealthy and unnatural. Brainwave patterns are altered, producing subtle psycho-chemical changes that are barely known or understood at the present time. The sleep is not deeply energizing because the senses are just chemically dulled out temporarily; they are never really off. The drugs result in increased levels of toxins in the bloodstream which drain the body of energy and lead to disease. We often don't remember our dreams on drugs because the physical body and mind are dulled out. Then the Body-Ego lies and tells us it was restful, calling the interval between passing out and regaining consciousness—"sleep." This is a vicious cycle because the body gets more and more uptight, fearful, anxiety-ridden, drained of energy and becomes ever more dependent.

This analysis doesn't only apply to "addicts"; it applies to those of us who from time to time "just smoke a joint," "take a sleeping pill," "take a drink," or whatever.

The only way out is to . . .

Chapter 15

EVERYTHING YOU WANTED TO KNOW ABOUT SLEEP BUT WERE TOO TIRED TO ASK

Better health means better sleep. Better sleep means better health. The two are inseparable.

Our sleep habits and how we feel after sleeping are a good barometer of our internal condition because high-quality sleep depends on many things such as physical health, proper mental attitude, and the ability of the Ego and senses to let go. These things in turn lead to (or represent) health and happiness.

Health means harmony within the physical body. Disease is a symptom of more impurities in the body tissue and bloodstream than the body can handle. The effort of the body to eliminate the impurities requires physical energy; this is why people often require more sleep when they are sick, particularly when high levels of foreign impurities are circulating in the bloodstream.

The mutual improvement of health and sleep is a gradual, cumulative process consisting of the body slowly ridding itself of the impurities which have accumulated within the body from years of poor eating and living habits.

Out mental attitude, outlook and feelings about ourselves impact greatly on our sleep. If we work hard, feel we have done a worthwhile job and are internally satisfied, sleep will be a welcomed, satisfying portion of our lives. If we feel hassled and bothered because there is "never enough time", then sleep will be an interruption. To think sleep is just a necessity to be tolerated is to be attached to our Egos and the life of the Senses. Sleep is as much an experience as anything else. Insomnia is due to restless action of the mind, unfulfilled desires and dissatisfaction with the self. Although western civilization likes to "cure" things (that is, "relieve symptoms,") with pills prescribed by "specialists," the cure for insomnia involves the whole being of an individual, so except for some drugs to chemically knock people out, the problem remains largely unsolved. The "cure" is to change the underlying life, because the barometer of sleep is usually quite accurate. This involves replacing dissatisfaction with self-satisfaction. Also methods of breath control and daily concentration can be utilized to remove the focus of the mind from the negative factors so that restorative sleep can occur.

PHYSICAL LOGISTICS OF SLEEP

This section contains some practical logistical suggestions you can use to gain maximum benefit and enjoyment from your sleep.

These logistical suggestions, if you have the will and character to follow them through the initial break-in period (during which things might actually seem worse), will quickly result in measurable improvement in your sleep and bodily condition while you work on the longer term factors such as Health and Mental Attitude.

1. **Pre-Sleep Procedures**

   Avoid eating, strenuous exercise and unnecessary mental activity within two hours of going to sleep.

2. **Hygiene**

   Wash your hands and face with soap and cool water. This cuts the vibrations of the day and relaxes the body and prepares it for sleep. Brush your teeth and thoroughly clear your nose and throat.

3. **Sleeping Surface**

   Beds, even the ones that are supposedly designed for a correct body posture for sleeping are a poor sleeping choice for several reasons:

   (a) Going to sleep in the same place every night is like a dog going to its doghouse.

   (b) Beds are dust-collectors and take up much space that could be more usefully employed.

   (c) They are not very happy for the back and spine, causing tremendous energy blockages leading to chronic pain.

The ideal sleeping surface.

A dusty, old bed is no better than a doghouse.

179

We recommend sleeping on a lightweight, portable foam mattress of the approximate dimensions shown.

When not in use during the day, the foam mattress can be rolled up along with blanket and pillow and conveniently stored.

You will find the whole vibration of sleeping becomes a lot lighter. In addition to being much better for you psychologically, you will find that if you want to sleep in another room or at a friend's house you can just take your bed with you. You can get rid of that funky, outdated dust collector that sits in the same place for years. In fact, you might consider getting rid of that unnecessary bed, too.

Don't be misled by the negative comments of people you know who might scoff at the idea without ever having even tried it. If you like, you can keep your bed and try the portable foam mattress. So consider getting rid of that bed! It's not exactly risking your life.

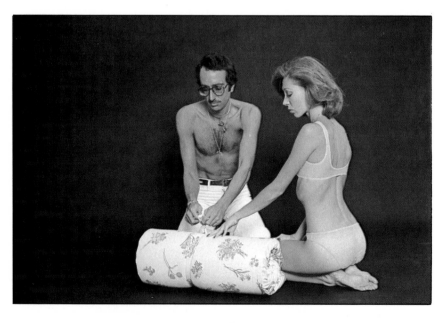

The Power Mat™ rolls up for easy storage after use

4. Sleep only on your back or on your left side. The reasons for this have to do with the location of the internal organs, particularly the heart and the liver. This may be difficult to do at first, but obviously if you stick with it, at some point you will be so tired that the body will do it. This will also help you achieve lighter dreams and breathe better while you are sleeping. If you wake up on your stomach or right side, tell yourself, consciously, not to do that and go back to sleep properly.

5. When falling asleep, use the dreem method of breath control.

Breathe in and out through your nose only. As you inhale say to yourself: "DREEEEE" (like the first part of the word dream with an extended "E" at the end that rises in pitch as the breath is drawn in). Inhale slowly, expanding the abdomen first and then the chest. Hold the breath for a while as the "E" sound in the mind continues to rise in pitch. Then exhale, beginning from the abdomen. As you exhale, mentally say the sound "MMMMMMM" (like in "hum" with an extended "M" with a sound that falls in pitch as you exhale). The DREEM sound that you make in your mind as you do the DREEM is the electromagnetic "sound" of your breathing. By learning to dwell on this mental sound instead of restlessly tossing and thinking about the events of day, your sleep will be much more beneficial to you.

FEEL GOOD NOW!

everything you always wanted

wants to help you
feel good

In order to make it possible for you to enjoy the benefits of the ideal sleep surface, without going through a big hassle, you may order a Power Mat™ directly from Dreamworld.

In addition to being a great sleeping surface, the Power Mat™ has many other uses. If you are traveling or camping, throw it in your suitcase or in the back of your car and you have a bed right there with you. (Total weight is only about four pounds.) If you go on a picnic or to the beach, take it with you. Use it as an extra bed when you have guests. Use it as a comfortable surface to exercise on, indoors or outdoors. The Power Mat™ also makes a most unique gift.

When not in use, the Power Mat™ is designed to be rolled up for easy, compact storage. The uses of the Power Mat™ are as unlimited as your imagination.

The Power Mat™ is recommended by doctors and others in the medical profession.

The Power Mat™ can be rolled and stored in any small, convenient area.

The Power Mat™ comes complete

Each Power Mat™ comes
ready to use, with
 • portable foam mattress
 • custom made mattress cover
 • matching pillowcase
 • matching tie-string

How to Get Yours

**Offer good only
while supplies last**

Don't deprive yourself of the many advantages of owning your own Power Mat™. To order, print your name and address on a piece of paper and send $32.95 (California residents add $1.98 sales tax) to:

Dreamworld
Computerized Processing Center
Box 67551
Los Angeles, CA 90067

No charge for postage, handling and shipping. To use Master Charge, Bankamericard or Visa, include your card number, expiration date and interbank number (if any) along with your name, address, and signature.

**Use your Power Mat™ as an extra bed when
unexpected company drops in.**

Chapter 16

FOUR STEPPES TO RELAXATION:
OR, STOP RUSSIAN AROUND

Rest and relaxation are very different things from "loafing," "laziness" or similar notions. On the contrary, those who have mastered the science of relaxation are usually the most active and energetic people, but they waste no energy, with them every motion counts.

In order to best comprehend relaxation, let us first consider its opposite: contraction. When we wish to contract a muscle in order that we may perform some action, we send an impulse from the brain to the muscle and the muscle contracts. The nerve energy travels over the motor nerves, reaches the muscle and causes it to draw its ends together and to thus exert a pull upon the part we wish to move. And so it is with every act of the body, conscious or unconscious. In the conscious act the conscious faculties send a message to the Instinctive Mind which immediately obeys the order by sending the current of nerve energy to the desired part. In the functions of the autonomous nervous systems (e.g., heart beat), the Instinctive Mind does not wait for orders, it attends to the whole work itself, both the ordering and the execution. But every action, conscious or unconscious, uses up a certain amount of "vital force" and if the amount so used is in excess of the amount which the system has been in the habit of storing, the result is that we feel weakened and generally "used up."

There is another form of dissipating vital force that may be less obvious. Many of us squander our vital force in the performance of unnecessary nervous gestures. This waste of energy is similar to the loss occasioned by the failure to turn off the faucet in the sink which results in water trickling away, hour after hour. Most of us allow our vital force to trickle away in just such a manner. Frowning, closing our lips tightly or any similar action of expressing our mental state in a physical action are wastes. So are such bad habits as tapping on the table or arms of chairs, twirling the thumbs, wiggling the fingers, tapping on the floor with our feet, and chewing gum. All these things and many others too numerous to mention are waste; pure waste; pure, pure waste. Pure, pure, pure, waste. Totally unnecessary. Yes, totally. Not anything but waste. Pure waste.

How many insidious energy wasting habits can you spot?

Uncontrolled thoughts cause an imperceptible current of nerve energy to flow, producing a slight muscular contraction and a consequent waste of energy.

A person possessed of a calm and controlled mind will have no such impulses with their accompanying negative results. Such a person moves along well poised. He is master, not slave.

In a state of relaxation, there is practically no current of nerve energy being emanated. A small amount is always being sent to the different parts of the body in order to maintain health, but this is a very small current compared to one sent out to contract a muscle. In relaxation the muscles and nerves are at rest and the vital force is conserved instead of being dissipated in reckless expenditures.

The lazy tramp is not an instance of relaxation; there is a great difference between relaxation and 'loafing'." The former is a sensible rest between working efforts, the result being that work is done better and with less effort— the latter is the result of a mental indisposition to work.

The person thus understanding relaxation and the conserving of energy accomplishes the best work. He does not expend useless energy or allow his strength to trickle away. Many of us, not understanding this, expand up from three to twenty times the energy necessary to do our work, be it physical or mental. If you doubt this statement, then spend a day watching the people with whom you come in contact and see how many wasted motions they make, and how many exaggerated movements they manifest. They do not have themselves under control mentally, and the result is physical waste.

Did you ever notice a cat in repose, or crawling before a mousehole? The cat crouches in an easy, graceful manner —with no muscular contraction and no tension, a beautiful picture of intense vitality in repose, but ready for instant action. Still and motionless it waits, to all appearances asleep, or even dead.

But watch when it moves! Like a flash of lightning it darts forward.

In fact, there can be no great power of quick and effective action unless the ability to relax is also there. People who fidget, fret, and fume are not the people who do the best work. They wear themselves out before the hour for action arrives. The person who may be depended upon is the one who possesses calmness, the ability to relax. The "fidgety" person need not despair; however, relaxation and repose may be cultivated by utilizing the EYAW Power Tools in combination with the Rules and Guidelines previously shown in this book.

This is not relaxation, this is the Cleveland Model Cities Program.

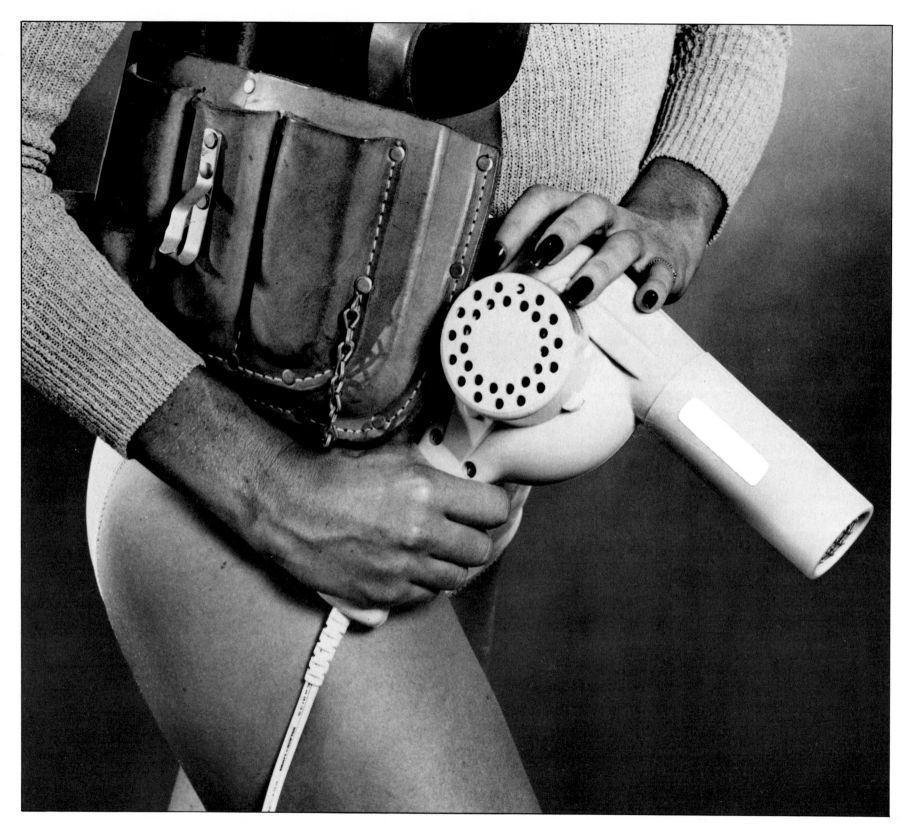

The EYAW Power Tools.

PRINCIPLES OF RELAXATION

Thoughts take form in action and actions react upon the mind. These two Truths stand together. We have heard much about the influence of the mind over the body, but we must not forget that the body, or its attitudes and positions, reacts upon the mind and influences mental states. We all know of the experiment of forcing a smile to the lips and eyes and maintaining it for a while, which generally results in making you "feel" "smiling" after a few minutes.

One of the first steps toward preventing the harmful practices of muscular contraction, with its resulting waste of vital force and wearing out of the nerves, is to cultivate a mental attitude of calmness and repose. This may be done, but it will be hard work at first; you will, however, be well paid for your trouble in the end. Mental poise and ease may be brought about by the eradication of worry and anger.

Anger is a sort of temporary insanity. It is pitiful to see a person lose control of himself and fly into a rage. Anger is a sign of weakness, a drain of personal power and nothing is accomplished by it. It is a useless waste of energy and a positive injury to the brain and nervous system.

Worry is a ridiculous dissipation of energy, and a totally self-indulgent ego-trip. Careful thought is desirable when problems have to be solved or obstacles surmounted, but there is never a need to descend to worry. Worrying is absolutely unnecessary. You can only change the things you can, and no amount of worry will change the things you can't. **Worrying is an excuse not to be powerful.**

Don't descend to worry.

187

POWER TOOL 1—"HEAVY AS LEAD"

Lie down flat on your back, close your eyes and relax as thoroughly as you can, letting go of all the muscles. Then, still relaxed, let your mind wander over the body from head down to toes. In doing this, you will find that here and there certain muscles are still in a tense condition; let go of them. If you do this thoroughly, you will end by having every muscle in the body fully relaxed and the nerves at rest. You will improve with practice as you learn for yourself, both physically and mentally, what "letting go" means. Take a few deep breaths, lying quietly and fully relaxed. While doing this exercise and lying relaxed, carry in your mind the thought that you are lying on a soft, downy couch and that your body and limbs are heavy as lead. Repeat the words (in your mind) several times "heavy as lead, heavy as lead."

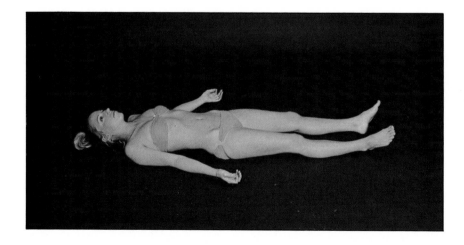

POWER TOOL 2—"LET GO"

Lie down on your back, with the soles of your feet on the ground and your knees in the air. Place the palms of your hands on either side of your head with the fingertips pointing towards your shoulders. Placing all your weight on the soles of your feet and your palms, push yourself up as shown below. Be sure to arch yourself as high as possible and arch your neck fully so you are looking down towards the floor.

POWER TOOL 3—"STRETCHING"

Stand on the floor with your legs apart and your arms spread apart and extended over your head. Then raise yourself on your toes and stretch yourself out gradually as if you were trying to reach the ceiling. This most simple exercise can be done any place and is wonderfully refreshing.

POWER TOOL 4—MENTAL RELAXATION

Sit or lie quietly in a relaxed, comfortable position and withdraw your mind as far as possible from outside objects and thoughts which require active mental effort. Let your mind reach inward and dwell upon the real self. Think of yourself as independent of the body and as able to leave it without impairing your individuality. You will gradually experience a feeling of peace and contentment. Attention must be withdrawn entirely from the physical body and centered entirely upon the higher "I," which is really "you." Think of the vast worlds around us, the millions of suns, each surrounded with its group of planets like our earth, only in many cases much larger. Get an idea of the immensity of space and of time; consider the extent of Life in all its forms on all these worlds and then realize the position of the earth and of yourself, a mere insect upon a speck of dirt. Then rise upward in your thought and realize that, though you be but an atom of the mighty whole, you are still a bit of Life itself, a particle of Wonderful Energy; that you are immortal, eternal, and indestructible; a necessary part of the Whole, a part which the Whole cannot get along without, a piece needed to fit into the structure of the Whole. Recognize yourself as in touch with all of Life; feel the Life of the Whole throbbing through you; the whole ocean of Life rocking you on its bosom. And then awake and return to your physical life and you will find that your body is refreshed, your mind calm and strong, and you will feel an inclination to do that piece of work which you have been putting off for so long. You have profited and been strengthened by your trip into the upper regions of the mind.

Chapter 17

BREATHING: A SOUND INVESTMENT IN THE FUTURE

Vital force in Air (not to be confused with the Air Force base in Vital, Colorado).

Life is absolutely dependent upon the act of breathing. Breath is life.

Breathing may be considered the most important of all the functions of the body, for, indeed, all the other functions depend on it. We may exist for a considerable time without eating, a shorter time without drinking, but without breathing our existence as a body may be measured by a few minutes.

And not only is man dependent upon breath for life, but he is largely dependent upon correct habits of breathing for continued vitality and freedom from disease. An intelligent control of our breathing power will lengthen our days on earth by giving us increased vitality and powers of resistance. Unintelligent and careless breathing will tend to shorten our days by decreasing our vitality and laying us open to disease.

Man in his natural state did not require instruction in breathing.

Each atom or group of atoms can be considered to be a "living thing" and thereby contains its own internal supply of "vital force." The air we breathe, the water we drink, and the food we eat are, of course, all groups of atoms and thereby contain such "vital force." The absorption of "vital force" from air, water, and food is the method by which we replenish our body's own supply of vital force.

Air, which is lighter vibrationally than water or solid food, is the medium through which the "vital force" can most readily be absorbed into the human body. So, correct breathing plays more than a physiological function in the human body, it also provides a major portion of the replenishment of the "vital force" without which life in a physical body cannot exist.

Air contains more than hydrogen, oxygen, and nitrogen, and something more important than oxygenation of the blood is accomplsihed by breathing. By rhythmical and proper breathing we may bring ourselves into harmonious vibrations with nature and greatly advance the unfoldment of our latent powers. By controlled breathing we may cure disease in ourselves and greatly reduce fear, worry, and other less desirable emotions.

mechanics of breathing . . .

In the art of inhalation (not to be confused with the Duke of Windsor), the diaphragm and muscle layers surrounding the lungs expand the lungs so that a vacuum is created and in accordance with the well-known law of physics, the air rushes in the body. Everything depends upon the muscles concerned with the process of respiration. Without the aid of these muscles, the lungs cannot expand. Power Breathing (described below) depends largely upon correct use and control of these respiratory muscles. The proper control of these muscles will result in the ability to attain the maximum degree of lung expansion to secure for the body the greatest amount of life giving properties in the air.

PROPER METHOD OF BREATHING
(THE POWER BREATH)

Learning to breathe properly is exceedingly important to our bodily health and mental development. The learning process is as physical as learning to play tennis or lifting weights. It requires work, time, and patience, but the results are great and no one who has attained them would willingly go back to the old methods. Start right and spectacular results will follow, neglect your foundations and sooner or later your entire building will topple over.

The mechanics of breathing.

inhalation...

Stand or sit erect and breathe through the nostrils only! (More about this later.)

Inhale steadily, first filling the lower part of the lungs which is accomplished by bringing into play the diaphragm, which when descending, exerts a gentle forward pressure on the abdominal organs, pushing forward the front walls of the abdomen. Then fill the middle portion of the lungs by pushing out the lower ribs, breast bone, and chest. Then fill the higher portion of the lungs, protruding the upper chest, thus lifting the upper chest including the upper ribs. In this final movement, the lower parts of the abdomen will be slightly drawn in: this movement giving the lungs a support and also helping to fill the highest part of the lungs with vital force.

At this point, the lungs are completely filled with a fresh supply of air. Most people today simply "breathe" by expanding the upper chest with the diaphragm rising instead of descending as the breath begins.

With practice these three steps of proper inhalation will be done in one continuous movement. Avoid a jerky series of inhalations and strive to attain a steady continuous action.

exhalation . . .

After completing Inhalation, retain the breath for a few seconds. Exhale slowly, holding the chest in a firm position and drawing the abdomen in a little and lifting it upward slowly as the air leaves the lungs. When the air is almost completely exhaled, relax the chest and abdomen.

A little practice will render this part of the exercise easy and the movement once acquired will be afterwards performed almost automatically.

At the beginning of practice, you may have some degree of difficulty in acquiring the Power Breath, but a little practice will make you perfect.

effects of correct power breathing . . .

Here's Joe Plotsky working his very first
Power Routine

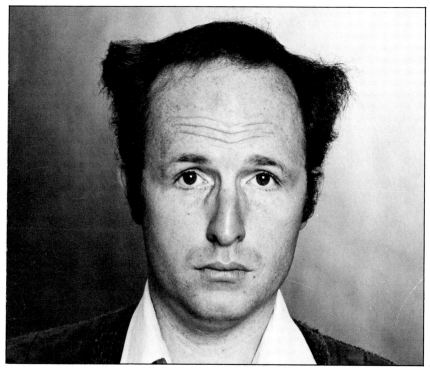

Here's Joe only ten days after getting
Everything You Always Wanted

As shown by the photos above, scarcely too much can be said of the advantages attending the practice of the EYAW Power Breathing Technique.

MASTERING THE EYAW POWER BREATH-
ING TECHNIQUES IS OF VITAL IMPOR-
TANCE TO EVERY MAN, WOMAN AND
CHILD.

SOME SIMPLE BREATHING EXERCISES

1. **The Power Breath**
   Practice as previously described.

2. **The Cleansing Breath**
   This form of breathing is excellent for ventilation and cleansing the lungs.
   (a) Inhale a complete breath
   (b) Retain the air for a few seconds
   (c) Pucker up the lips as if to whistle (but do not swell out the cheeks). Then exhale a little air through the opening with considerable vigor. Then stop for a moment, retaining the air, and then exhale a little more air. Repeat until the air is completely exhaled. Remember that considerable vigor is to be used in exhaling the air through the opening in the lips. The breath will be found quite refreshing when one is tired and generally "used up."

3. **The Retained Breath**
   This is a very important exercise which tends to strengthen and develop the respiratory muscles as well as the lungs. Frequent practice will also tend to expand the chest.

   Pay considerable attention to this exercise as it is easy and has great merits:
   (a) Stand erect.
   (b) Inhale an EYAW Power Breath.
   (c) Retain the air as long as you can comfortably.
   (d) Exhale vigorously through the open mouth.
   (e) Practice the Cleansing Breath.

   At first you will be able to retain the breath only a short time, but a little practice will show a great improvement. Time yourself with a watch if you wish to note your progress.

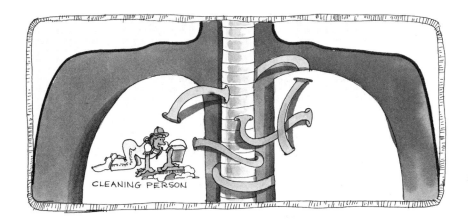

nostril breathing vs mouth breathing . . .

Our breathing mechanism is so constructed that we may breathe either through the mouth or nasal tubes, but it is a matter of vital importance to us which method we follow, as one brings health and strength and the other, disease and weakness.

The proper method of breathing is to take the breath through the nostrils, but we find people in all walks of life habitually breathing through their mouths.

Many contagious diseases are contracted by the senseless habit of mouth breathing. Carefully conducted scientific experiments have shown that soldiers and sailors who sleep with their mouths open are much more liable to contract contagious diseases then those who breathe properly through their nostrils.

Using your mouth improperly can be hazardous to your heatlh.

200

One who habitually breathes through the nostrils is not likely to be troubled with clogged or stuffy nostrils, but for the benefit of those who have become more or less addicted to the unnatural habit of mouth breathing and who wish to acquire the natural and rational method, we offer the following methods regarding the way to keep the nostrils clean and free from impurities.

Sniff a little water up the nostrils, allowing it to run down the passages into the throat from where it may be ejected or just let it run back out of your nose if you want to start with something easy. Also blowing the nose after sniffing water into the nostrils will remove impurities and thus clear the nasal passages.

Another good plan is to open the window and breathe freely, closing one nostril with the finger or thumb, sniffing up the air through the open nostril. Then repeat the process on the other nostril. Do this several times. This will usually clean the nose of obstructions.

We again emphasize the importance of acquiring the proper method of breathing and caution against dismissing this phase of the subject matter as unimportant.

The organs of respiration have their only protective apparatus, filter, or dust catcher in the nostrils. When the breath is taken in through the mouth, there is nothing from the mouth to the lungs to strain the air or to catch the dust and other foreign matter in the air. From mouth to lungs, the dirt or impure substance has a clean track and the entire respiratory system is unprotected. Moreover, such incorrect breathing admits cold air to the respiratory organs, thereby injuring them.

The nostrils are long narrow chambers containing numerous bristly hairs which serve the purpose of a filter to strain the air of its impurities. This is particularly important to city dwellers who live in environments containing a high degree of pollution and impurities. The nostrils also warm the inhaled air.

Another feature of mouth breathing is that the nasal passages, being comparatively unused, consequently fail to keep themselves clean and clear and become clogged up, unclean, and are likely to contract local disease. Like abandoned roads that soon become filled with weeds and rubbish, unused nostrils become filled with impurities and foul matter.

Chapter 18

ASTRAL FLIGHTS:
YOUR KEY TO ULTIMATE POWER

Astral flights are the other subcomponent of the Dream State. Unlike dreaming, which involves no conscious control, the basic characteristics of an astral flight is conscious control and perception. During astral flights, we have our full frontal consciousness without the excess baggage of the material body and the five body senses. It is like being in a dream, but being awake and conscious; that is, it is like being in the waking state, but on a non-material level—just as the electromagnetic body is awake and alive on a non-material level after death.

In dreaming, the electromagnetic body is still centered in the physical body which is unconscious. In an astral flight, the electromagnetic body is not centered in the physical body but we retain that which we identify as our waking state "Consciousness." To one who has not experienced an astral flight it is difficult to describe the difference between that and dreaming. In an astral flight we can motivate, redirect and change direction just as we can in the Waking State with the additional advantage that we are not bored by the slow heavy constraints of material time and space. (Remember how hard it is to get to New York from Los Angeles in the Waking State.) Astral flights are sometimes called "out of body experiences" because that is exactly what happens. The electromagnetic body physically projects itself out of its centered position in the physical body. Astral levels are spaces of energy, not matter, though they are just as "real" (or unreal).

How To Have An Astral Flight

Before you go to sleep, concentrate on seeing yourself, as your physical body in a "dream" and remembering it when you "wake up." This is not easy to do at first. Once you have enough control to see yourself consciously in a dream and remember it, it means that your electromagnetic body has separated from your physical body and you can begin to direct your electromagnetic body through the astral levels without the need of dragging the heavy physical body around as a vehicle as we must do here on the earth plane. This may seem strange at first, but you needn't worry. When you "wake up," it means that your electromagnetic body has recentered itself in the physical body and everything proceeds as before except you feel very relaxed, fresh, and happy. Most often, we return to the physical body without a conscious effort. We suddenly just "realize" we are back in our bodies. **(If we realize we are more than our physical body and we think about whether we choose to return to it, we have achieved immortality then and there because we have proven to ourselves that we have an existence and a consciousness having nothing to do with our physical bodies.)**

Even if we come back to the body, we realize in a personal "knowing" way, instead of just dry, intellectual thinking that we are not the body and we actually have a choice as to whether or not we desire to have the real us reside on the physical plane or exist on the level of electromagnetics. As we learn to consciously direct our Astral Flights . . .

WE BECOME
AWARE OF CONDITIONS BEFORE
THEY EXIST. WE BECOME THE MAS-
TER OF OUR DESTINY.

**THEREFORE,
GAINING CONTROL OVER OUR
DREAM STATES SO WE HAVE CON-
TROLLED ASTRAL FLIGHTS IN-
STEAD OF DULL, USELESS DREAMS
IS AT LEAST INVALUABLE.**

As you might expect, however, nothing good comes easy, except "Everything You Always Wanted."

For most people, success in having Astral Flights depends upon excellent physical health, internal body cleanliness, a clear, happy attitude, and proper physical sleeping habits.

While you are working on these things, or even if you decide not to attempt them, try to see yourself fully in a dream, then remember it when you awaken, and you will be on the right road.

To order additional copies of "Everything You Always Wanted"™ for yourself or friends, send $14.95 per copy + $1.00 per copy for postage & shipping (California residents add $.90 per copy sales tax) to:

DREAMWORLD™
Computerized Processing Center
Box 67551
Los Angeles, California 90067

offer good only while supplies last